MY GENERATION

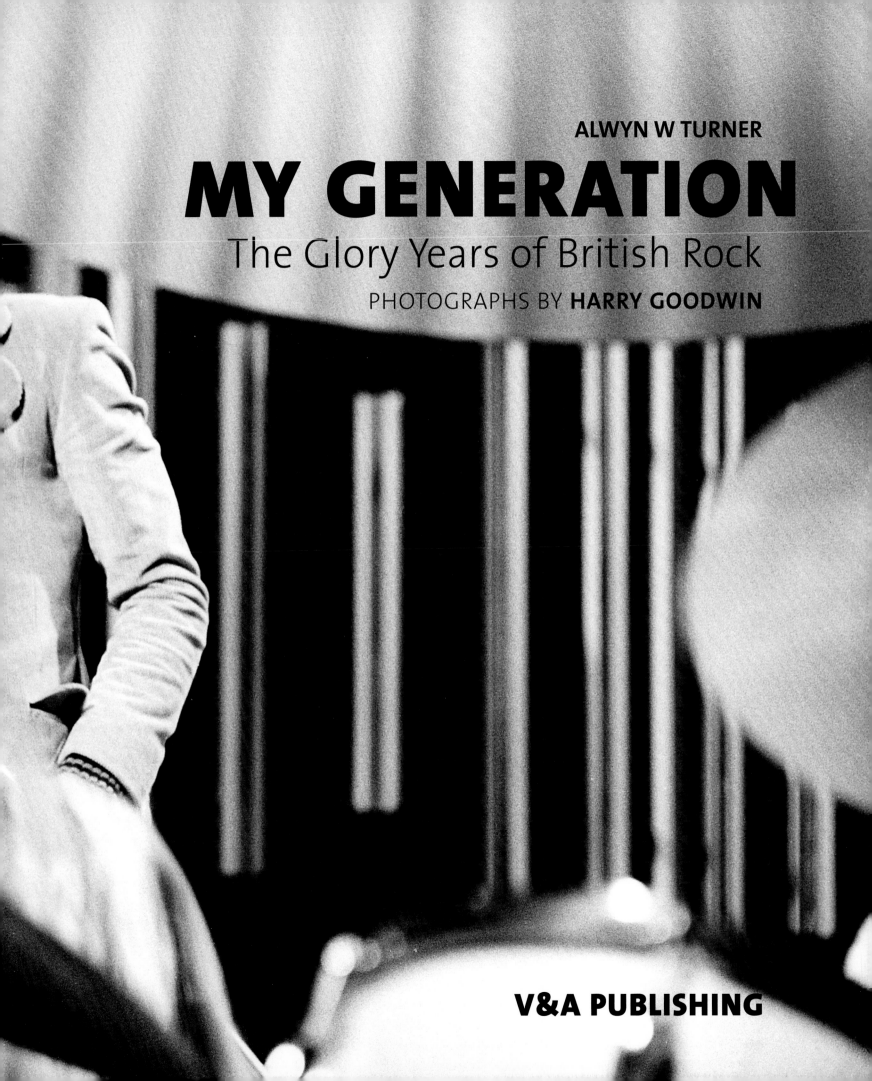

ALWYN W TURNER

MY GENERATION

The Glory Years of British Rock

PHOTOGRAPHS BY **HARRY GOODWIN**

V&A PUBLISHING

Contents

TOP OF THE POP PHOTOGRAPHERS

During the instrumental break in the Kinks' 1970 song 'Top of the Pops', a disembodied voice, with a slightly unconvincing attempt at a Mancunian accent, can be heard exclaiming, 'Shot of a lifetime, is that!' The reference would have been lost on most of those hearing the song but to anyone who knew Harry Goodwin – and that meant anyone who'd ever appeared on the BBC television's most popular and long-lived pop music show *Top of the Pops* – it was instantly familiar. For Goodwin was the resident photographer on that programme for its first ten years and 'Shot of a lifetime!' was one of his catchphrases, uttered after capturing the image he was after; alternatives included the equally exuberant claims: 'It's a winner!' and 'That's a Rembrandt!' The contagious enthusiasm was characteristic of a man who became an integral part of a national institution.

Harry Goodwin was born in Manchester on 21 July 1924, the son of a bookmaker, Jack Goodwin, who worked principally at the Belle Vue greyhound stadium, and after leaving school Harry joined him, learning the trade of the tic-tac man. Sport was his first and most abiding love: 'You had to be able to look after yourself at the track, so I boxed at a decent level from a young age and could have gone pro as a footballer.' As with so many others of his generation, however, his plans were thrown into confusion with the outbreak of the Second World War. The family moved to Blackpool to escape the bombing raids and it was there, at the age of eighteen, that he was conscripted into the RAF and sent to India. Or, as he puts it, 'I got caught up in that Japanese war.'

He served for seven years, during which time were planted the seeds of his future career. Wanting to ensure that this talented young sportsman had enough leisure time to sort out the unit's football team, his sergeant moved him from general duties to the photography section. Thus was realized one of Goodwin's early ambitions: 'I was always keen to have a go with a camera because I'm a

OPPOSITE: Harry Goodwin and Peter Noone (photograph by Ron Howard).

OPPOSITE: Harry Goodwin's first commercial shoot – comedian Ken Dodd promoting milk.

great believer that if you've got a camera, you can always get friendly with the girls.' And although his early work was centred on loading cameras for photographers engaged in reconnaissance flights over Japanese-occupied territory in Burma, the ending of the war provided precisely those opportunities: 'When we were moved to Kuala Lumpur, I'd borrow their equipment and take pictures of some of the local girls and flog the pictures to the lads. That was my first paid work as a photographer.'

Harry Goodwin's first ever photograph: his brother Bill in Blackpool.

When asked what the RAF taught him about photography, Goodwin is dismissive: 'Nothing. I learnt the hard way,' he says. 'I've never read a book about photography or taken a course. It just came to me naturally and I learned the rest on the job.'

Returning to Manchester after being de-mobbed, he became a freelance photographer, with his first commission being shots of the footballer Ephraim 'Jock' Dodds, whose career – though badly affected by the war – included a famous hat-trick for Scotland against England; Dodds was to become a lifelong friend. Primarily, though, Goodwin spent the 1950s working at beauty pageants and on the boxing circuit, and frequenting the clubs of the Northwest. When Frank Taylor, the stage manager of the Hulme Hippodrome, one of his regular haunts, moved to the BBC studios in Dickenson Road, Manchester, he suggested to Goodwin that he apply there for casual labour. And so, at the start of the 1960s, he began to supplement his photographic income with work as a scene shifter, assisting on shows that featured the usual diversity of BBC talent, from the Northern Dance Orchestra to comedian Harry Worth to the puppet pigs Pinky and Perky. The *Radio Times*, then the country's biggest selling magazine, also began to feature some of his photographs, which he developed in a darkroom that had been converted from an old back room at his home by his brother Jack.

In late 1963 he was approached about a new six-part series to be titled *Top of the Pops*. 'They needed someone to photograph the bands. When the producer, Johnnie Stewart, came up from London, he thought I was streetwise and a hustler. So he gave me the job.'

The job stretched out from its projected six-week duration and was to last from the beginning of 1964 to the end of 1973, a decade in which every major pop star in the world, with the sole exception of Elvis Presley, was to appear on the programme. And every one of them was photographed by Goodwin, from the Beatles and the Rolling Stones, through Bob Dylan and Jimi Hendrix, to David Bowie and Rod Stewart. At a time when the British pop scene was at its absolute height of popularity and influence, *Top of the Pops* became the single most important programme in the industry, capable of making stars literally overnight. Its significance was not restricted to British acts, for its national reach in such an important market, capable not merely of generating sales but of shaping international taste, was the envy of American stars, who queued up to appear.

When filming moved in 1966 from Manchester to London, Goodwin kept his job, at the insistence he says of Stewart, who had to 'fight tooth and nail to get the top brass to allow my services to be retained'. The new location required a search to find an assistant with a darkroom, capable of the rapid turnaround needed for the show. Given the professional rivalry of the capital's photographers, it was a far from easy task, but at the last minute he found Ron Howard, with whom he was to remain for many years – Ron's wife, Joyce, also assisted with the retouching of the photographs. The move also necessitated a weekly commute: 'When I went to London on the train,' he later recalled, 'I used to look at all the houses with the aerials on their roofs and I thought: it's up to me what they're going to get tonight. I felt powerful. It was a marvellous feeling.'

Goodwin's unique position – on a show that was itself unique – enabled him to build a portfolio spanning a range of artists that was probably greater than that of any other rock photographer. As Bee Gee Barry Gibb said: 'He's a legend. I don't think there's any artist who hasn't been photographed by this man.'

His approach was summed up by fellow photographer John O'Connor, who learned his trade with Goodwin: 'Get in, get out, don't be part of the wallpaper; don't hang around and people will ask you back again.' Goodwin himself observes that 'It's not about taking pictures, it's about getting people to work with you,' and his positive manner won over most of his subjects. 'He became a friend,' said Gerry Marsden of Gerry and the Pacemakers. 'We would always do whatever nonsense he requested,' added Peter Noone of Herman's Hermits. 'He made us laugh and made us all totally at ease, which in retrospect is what all the great artist photographers must have done. He was a gent.' And his contribution to the show was recognized by those who worked on it. 'His self-inflicted job', remarked *Top of the Pops* presenter Jimmy Savile, 'was that he had to calm down all the people in the studio.'

Stevie Wonder, Motown's most influential artist, was one of many American stars to perform on *Top of the Pops* and be photographed by Harry Goodwin.

ABOVE AND RIGHT: Mick Jagger with the men who made
Top of the Pops a success: its creator, Johnnie Stewart (right)
and its first presenter, Jimmy Savile (above).

It was an approach that paid repeated dividends. When Goodwin first photographed the Beatles, he discovered that 'John Lennon could be a right one,' but after the band split up, he was surprised to receive an invitation to take solo shots of the ex-Beatle. 'I wondered why he'd asked for me and I was a bit nervous. Then he introduced me to Yoko as the greatest photographer in Britain. It shocked me but then I realized I didn't make him feel uncomfortable.' Some of those shots were later to be put on permanent exhibition at John Lennon Airport in Liverpool.

There were some encounters that proved more abrasive, including Dylan at his uncooperative worst, though as Goodwin later reflected, 'I still got the shots needed for the show with hours to spare.' He also got into an argument with Brian Jones of the Rolling Stones on the first ever edition of *Top of the Pops*, though the altercation soon turned to friendship, particularly when Jones discovered that Goodwin had taken photographs of the blues legend Sonny Boy Williamson. And then there was Dusty Springfield. 'Dusty was the most difficult person,' he said: 'Five pictures in five years I got off her; she was an absolute perfectionist. But what an amazing talent!' Despite the problems, the resultant photographs have become amongst the most iconic images of the artists involved, as have his more easily acquired shots of Jimi Hendrix and Aretha Franklin, both of which appeared on the cover of *Rolling Stone* magazine.

After leaving *Top of the Pops*, Goodwin continued to work in the pop field into the 1980s, exploiting his extensive range of contacts for the benefit of magazines like *Jackie*, *Blue Jeans* and *Patches*, and moving on to a new generation of bands, from the Jam to Joy Division. Even more to his taste, he was also commissioned by the BBC sports programme *Grandstand*, for whom he toured the Scottish football clubs. It was there that he first encountered Alex Ferguson, who was managing Aberdeen at the time; when Ferguson moved to Manchester United in 1986, eventually to become the most successful club manager ever in British football, another long-term relationship was cemented. 'I think the important issue was the trust that he brought to the job,' noted Ferguson. 'He had the knack with people and still does.' He was also one of the very few photographers with whom the enigmatic French player Eric Cantona was happy to work, 'because Harry makes me laugh.' And for a young generation of Manchester boxers, he represented an unbroken link with the past, as the world light-welterweight champion Ricky Hatton pointed out: 'He's mixed in very high company. He's been around Muhammad Ali, Joe Frazier, John Conteh, Joe Louis.'

The *Top of the Pops* studio.

Harry Goodwin with
Muhammad Ali (photograph
by Ron Howard).

It is, however, for the portraits of pop stars that Harry Goodwin is principally celebrated. The photographs for *Top of the Pops* were taken in order to be used in the chart rundown that preceded the playing of the week's #1 single. They were thus intended to be seen for only a second or two, just long enough for the presenter to read out the name of the artist, the song title and the chart position, and even then they were mostly experienced via the primitive black-and-white television technology of the 1960s. They were regarded as being as instant and disposable as the performances on the programme and indeed as pop music itself. And yet they have survived – in some cases as the sole record of the artist's appearance on the show, for most of the early tapes of the programme were subsequently wiped – with their status enhanced by the passing years. The brief to which Goodwin was working suited his style perfectly: these are not the moody, shadow-draped images of rock and roll mythology, but clear, calm pictures of stars as people, often caught in the mundane reality of backstage: the Stones in the BBC canteen, the Equals crammed together in a corridor, surrounded by pipes and cables, the leather-clad, guitar-toting Thin Lizzy outside their dressing room.

Goodwin's emergence as one of the most celebrated rock photographers had been unexpected and entirely fortuitous. 'My dad was always very keen on me being a photographer some day,' he says. 'He wanted me on the promenade at Blackpool.' To some degree, that was precisely what he went on to do, except that his promenade was the *Top of the Pops* studio and instead of holidaymakers, his subjects were some of the most famous men and women of the age. But the essential attitude remained, the desire to put people at their ease, to make them feel part of a great and continuing tradition. In Jimmy Savile's words: 'Nobody ever forgot Harry.'

The immediacy of the shots places them firmly within pop music, not studies from outside but a vital part of the era, sharing with pop the evocative directness that Noel Coward referred to as 'the potency of cheap music'. As Goodwin's hero, the comedian Ken Dodd once noted: 'He's a recorder, he's a person who gets moments in time.'

chapter one

FERRY ACROSS THE MERSEY

In the early evening of New Year's Day 1964, while the independent television network was busy with local news, the only BBC channel then available screened the first episode of a new series entitled *Top of the Pops*. Broadcast live from a converted church in Dickenson Road, Manchester, the 25-minute programme had no great expectations vested in it and was scheduled to run for just six weeks. But, perhaps more by luck than judgement, the BBC had stumbled upon a winning formula, and the show proved so popular that it lasted for more than two thousand episodes, spanning 42 years, as it became one of the longest running series in British television history and easily outlived its early rivals, *Thank Your Lucky Stars*, *Juke Box Jury* and *Ready Steady Go!*

Both the timing and the location of the show were fortuitous. The year just ended had seen sales of singles and albums reach an all-time high, with British acts in the ascendency for the first time since the introduction of the charts in 1952: fourteen of the seventeen #1 singles in 1963 were home-grown (the exceptions came from Frank Ifield and Elvis Presley), with a strong emphasis on acts from northwest England – records by the Beatles, Gerry and the Pacemakers, the Searchers, and Billy J. Kramer and the Dakotas all reached the top that year. The creative centre of gravity in the domestic recording industry, hitherto fixed firmly in the songwriting and publishing networks of London's Tin Pan Alley, was no longer as secure as it had been, and the choice of Manchester as a venue for the new programme (although made for budgetary reasons) seemed to reflect a general drift northwards.

The business of actually making records continued to be a London-based activity, but the talent scouts of the record companies were now seldom to be seen in the capital. Instead they spent their time chasing around the clubs of Liverpool, Manchester, Birmingham and beyond in a fevered search for new

OPPOSITE: Adam Faith.

OPPOSITE: Cliff Richard, the biggest British star of the pre-Beatles era, who continued to thrive through the 1960s.

Chuck Berry, whose profile rose in Britain after being covered by the Beatles and the Rolling Stones.

scenes and new bands. 'The beat scene had loads of clubs in the centre of town,' remembered Manchester musician C.P. Lee. 'I counted well over two hundred.' Typical of many northern clubs was the Downbeat in Newcastle, where journalist Nik Cohn used to watch the Alan Price Combo (later known as the Animals): 'It was stuck on top of some kind of disused warehouse, down towards the docks, and the railway bridge ran right outside it, making it shake. It was cramped, wet, ratty and music made its walls buckle. And it was a fierce atmosphere, it burned.'

Such venues had been thriving for several years – Liverpool in particular had been sufficiently strong to sustain its own newspaper, *Mersey Beat*, since 1961, giving its name to the local scene – but it took the abrupt arrival of the Beatles, fresh from the Cavern Club, to shake up the record industry, suggesting that it had been ignoring the rest of the country for too long.

In fact rock and roll was slightly behind similar movements in other areas of culture. The tendency to look beyond London for artistic inspiration had already become evident, for example, in the theatrical renaissance that produced works such as Shelagh Delaney's *A Taste of Honey* (1958) and Arnold Wesker's *Roots* (1959), introducing Salford and Norfolk accents respectively to the stage. The cinema had offered adaptations of Nottingham-born Alan Sillitoe's novels *Saturday Night and Sunday Morning* and *The Loneliness of the Long-Distance Runner* (filmed in 1960 and 1962 respectively), while two of the most popular television drama series, *Coronation Street* (first broadcast in 1960) and *Z-Cars* (first broadcast in 1962), were set in Lancashire. Even in the small circles of pop television, the sensation of 1962 had been Janice Nicholls, a teenager from the Black Country who appeared as a critic of new singles on *Thank Your Lucky Stars* and turned 'Oi'll give it foive' into a national catchphrase.

LEFT: The Everly Brothers, whose harmonies were
a major influence on British bands.

Two American stars who covered British songs:
Del Shannon (left) had the first American hit with a
Beatles song, 'From Me to You', and Gene Pitney (right)
recorded 'That Girl Belongs to Yesterday', written by
Mick Jagger and Keith Richards.

Gene Vincent (top) remained a popular act in Britain, while Hank B. Marvin (above) continued to lead the Shadows to chart success right through the beat era.

OPPOSITE: Little Richard, who toured Britain in 1963, supported by the Rolling Stones.

If the artistic and broadcasting establishment was becoming aware that not everything of interest originated in the Southeast, there was also a feeling that the nation was somehow on the cusp of change, even if the nature of that change could not yet be readily identified. The years of austerity and post-war rationing were fast receding in the public memory, fast enough that the prime minister, Harold Macmillan, could assert that 'most of our people have never had it so good' and, rather than invite derision, lead the Conservative Party in 1959 to a third successive general election victory. This was a time of unprecedented affluence, with rapid rises in living standards, but the good times came at the price of what some perceived to be a certain stagnation, a complacency that required pricking; in 1961 the comedy revue *Beyond the Fringe* became a hit on the West End stage and proceeded to do just that.

The resultant satire craze arrived on television the following year with the BBC series *That Was the Week That Was*, presented by David Frost in a suburban grammar-school accent that was in its own way as radical as the northern voices being heard elsewhere. Initial ambitions went no higher than amusing a cult following (it was envisaged as 'late-night ghetto television which would probably only attract a fringe metropolitan audience', remembered the show's producer, Ned Sherrin), but within a couple of months there were 12 million people staying up on a Saturday night to watch the follies and failures of the establishment being held up to ridicule, a task that was admittedly made easier by a number of own-goals, from the unsuccessful prosecution of D.H. Lawrence's novel *Lady Chatterley's Lover* through to the Profumo affair. *That Was the Week That Was* was first broadcast in the same month that the Beatles entered the top 30 with their debut single, 'Love Me Do', and there were those who, in retrospect, connected the satire and beat booms. 'We had the same timing as the Beatles and challenged the same conventions,' noted Jonathan Miller, one of the stars of *Beyond the Fringe*. 'In a way you could say that the Beatles were satirical, or at least sceptical.'

The sense of imminent change in the country was emphasized with the death of Hugh Gaitskell, leader of the Labour Party, in January 1963. His successor, the man destined to become the next prime minister, was Harold Wilson, a member of parliament for, appropriately enough, a Liverpool constituency. His taste in Gannex raincoats may not have had much in common with youth fashion, but he was at least the right side of 50 (he was 22 years younger than Macmillan), and he did talk of the need for national renewal: 'Our young men and women have in their hands the power to change the world,' he declared excitedly. 'We want the youth of Britain to storm the new frontiers of knowledge.'

PREVIOUS PAGES: Roy Orbison
with (right) Stan Dorfman,
who would later become
producer of *Top of the Pops*,
filming a piece for the show
in the roof gardens of
the Derry & Toms store
in London.

RIGHT: The Beatles in their
one live appearance on
Top of the Pops, 16 June 1966.

The Beatles. Clockwise from top left: Paul McCartney, Ringo Starr, George Harrison, John Lennon.

The Beatles during a rehearsal for a television appearance.

The emphasis on youth – it was Wilson's government that was to reduce the voting age from twenty-one to eighteen later in the decade – was deliberate and characteristically opportunist. By 1964 there were 6 million teenagers in Britain, more than there had ever been before, and a recognizably distinct culture was emerging, one that cut across classes and identified itself exclusively with age. An inchoate demand for cultural democracy was forcing itself onto the public agenda. No longer were the young prepared to look like 'lamb dressed as mutton', as journalist Maureen Cleave put it, or to defer to their elders in matters of fashion and taste. 'Young people are the trendsetters,' argued John Stephen, the man who had brought boutiques to Carnaby Street in the West End of London. 'Why are they trendsetters? Lots of them don't have a lot of money and consequently what they have already bought, they attempt to adapt, to change the style, and from this we get new trends which we follow up in our shops.'

Johnny Pearson (above left) was conductor of the *Top of the Pops* Orchestra, while Robin Nash (above right) took over from Johnnie Stewart as the programme's producer.

OPPOSITE: Presenter Jimmy Savile riding his bicycle to the original *Top of the Pops* studio in Manchester.

OPPOSITE: *Top of the Pops* presenter Pete Murray with Samantha Juste. It was Juste's job to play the records to which the acts mimed; she later married Micky Dolenz of the Monkees.

Johnnie Stewart, the first producer of *Top of the Pops*.

Times were changing and all that was lacking was a central focus, a standard around which disparate forces could unite. It came with the Beatles.

The impact of the Beatles in 1963 was extraordinary. They ended the year with their third consecutive #1 hit, having achieved the two biggest selling singles of the year, with their second album also at #1 (continuing a 51-week unbroken run for them at the top), with eulogies to their work in the serious press, and with the word 'Beatlemania' freshly minted to describe their reception by fans. Beyond the music, however, was the social impact. It was as though they had caught all the straws that had been blowing in the wind over the last five years or so, and built from them a single image of young Britain, so strong that it would come to identify the decade. 'Suddenly people from Liverpool with money were acceptable,' remembered Peter Noone of Herman's Hermits. 'Before that, if you didn't have the right accent in England you were fucked. But after the Beatles it was suddenly cool to be a friend of the common people.' Similarly, the irreverence and humour with which they conducted interviews, under-cutting all established conventions of light entertainment, echoed the iconoclasm of the satirists. Certainly it was hard to imagine that Cliff Richard, their precursor as Britain's biggest rock act, would have been as rude about any of his contemporaries as they were about him: 'We've always *hated* him,' said John Lennon in 1964. 'He was everything we hated in pop.'

Few expressed such reservations about the Beatles. Even business rivals were more keen to express admiration and envy: they were 'simultaneously omniscient and naïve', said Andrew Loog Oldham, who managed the Rolling Stones. 'People said their image was that of the boy next door, but it wasn't,' remarked Simon Napier-Bell, manager of the Yardbirds. 'It was the cool, cocky brashness of a kid who's found a sugar-daddy and got himself set up in Mayfair.' More impressive still was

their adoption by the establishment, complete with endorsement from the Duke of Edinburgh: 'It seems to me that these blokes are helping people to enjoy themselves.' By December 1963 the Western Theatre Ballet was premiering in London its new piece *Mods and Rockers*, a variation on *West Side Story* to the accompaniment of Beatles songs; as the *Times* reviewer put it: 'Like it or lump it, the Liverpudlian quartet has introduced a new and distinctive sound into British pop music, which is significant because it no longer derives directly from American models.'

This last comment was not strictly true. At this point the Beatles' music did in fact derive very clearly from America. In common with that of many other Merseybeat groups, it drew on the anarchic energy of Little Richard, the guitars of Chuck Berry and the Everly Brothers, the vocal innovations of Buddy Holly, the gospel-derived call-and-response of girl groups and Tamla Motown. These influences were then blended into a new form, which, like the newly fashionable painters of Pop Art (with whom the Beatles were now rubbing shoulders in the glossy magazines), celebrated the culture of mass-consumerism, creating a montage of musical styles. 'They put together the rockabilly scene,' said Roger McGuinn of the Byrds; 'they mixed it with blues and bossa nova and classical and all kinds of influences. They kind of made a stew of all these different forms of music.' What was singularly absent from their early set lists, when they were playing predominantly cover versions, though, was the music of the first British rockers – Cliff Richard, Billy Fury, Johnny Kidd – as if a deliberate decision had been made to go straight to the source, unfiltered and unadulterated. Instead, both the Beatles and the practitioners of Pop Art looked primarily to America for their inspiration.

The Dave Clark Five. From left to right: Denis Payton, Mike Smith, Lenny Davidson, Rick Huxley, Dave Clark.

For the image of America remained the great fantasy of British popular
culture, the promised land of Hollywood, glamour and real stardom. No British
pop act had made a truly successful crossing of the Atlantic – the closest having
been Lonnie Donegan, who had achieved two top ten singles, albeit with a five-
year gap between – and there seemed no particular reason to expect the Beatles
to be any different.

There were some indications, however, that America was becoming more open
to British influences than it had been for many years. A number of photographers
(David Bailey, Terence Donovan, Brian Duffy) were making names for themselves
in the fashion industry; the new wave cinema was exporting successfully, with Oscar
nominations for Laurence Harvey in *Room at the Top* (1959) and Laurence Olivier in
The Entertainer (1960); and critics were talking about the 'British domination of
Broadway', as *Beyond the Fringe* and a team from the Establishment comedy club
enjoyed successful runs in New York in 1962, alongside Harold Pinter's play *The
Caretaker* and Anthony Newley's musical *Stop the World – I Want to Get Off*, with

OPPOSITE: Freddie Garrity of Manchester band Freddie and the Dreamers.

Lionel Bart's *Oliver!* not far behind. As John Mortimer was to put it in *Paradise Postponed* (1985), his novel of post-war Britain, for a brief moment: 'life in England was thought to be interesting to the American public.'

Again the Beatles were perfectly positioned to catch the wave. At the start of 1964 'I Want to Hold Your Hand' entered the American top 40 and, boosted by a heavily publicized and wildly received visit, reached #1 in February. By the end of the next month, the group were occupying all top five places in the charts, it was being estimated that they accounted for 60 per cent of all singles sales, and *Billboard* magazine was conceding defeat: 'Just about everyone is tired of the Beatles,' it admitted, 'except the buying public.' Thereafter, the floodgates opened, and where 1963 had seen just one record by a British act reach the American top ten, this rose to 34 in 1964, with a deluge of British bands following in the Beatles' wake. Amongst them were several acts who proved even more successful in America than at home: Herman's Hermits, Peter and Gordon and the Dave Clark Five. The latter, coming from North London, had evolved separately from the others, with instrumentation that featured sax and organ, and the Tottenham Sound was briefly talked up as an alternative to Merseybeat, the first of many such mirages as the media desperately chased after the next fad.

Cilla Black, who came out of Merseybeat to become one of Britain's biggest television stars.

In Britain too, 1964 was a success story for the industry. Singles sales again hit a new peak (they then fell off and didn't return to the same level for more than a decade) and fourteen different British acts reached #1 in the charts. Amidst the excitement, there were few dissenting voices, though journalist Paul Johnson, in a famous *New Statesman* diatribe, 'The Menace of Beatlism', did express his horror at pop fans: 'the huge faces, bloated with cheap confectionery and smeared with chain-store makeup, the open, sagging mouths and glazed eyes, the hands mindlessly drumming in time to the music, the broken stiletto heels, the shoddy, stereotyped "with-it" clothes'. But his was a minority position, and the sheer energy of the music, together with the scale of the profits, swept such doubters away.

This was the world into which *Top of the Pops* was launched. The initiative had come from Bill Cotton, the head of variety on BBC Television, who was later to explain that its genesis lay in the success of a rival ITV show: '*Ready Steady Go!* was doing amazing things. It was enjoying great success, and a lot of TV people and members of the public were being affected by it. However, I saw something in a show that merely reflected the biggest selling singles of the day; it seemed simple and right.' Cotton appointed producer Johnnie Stewart, who in turn chose the Radio Luxembourg disc jockey Jimmy Savile to host the show. Both Stewart and Savile separately claimed credit for the programme's title, although it was not entirely original – there had been a BBC radio show on the Light Programme back in 1956 with the same name, and the phrase had passed sufficiently into the language to be used in a *Times* editorial on the eve of Harold Wilson's first party conference as leader the previous autumn: 'Mr Wilson is and always has been top of the pops with conference delegates.'

Gerry Marsden of Gerry and the Pacemakers, the second biggest Merseybeat band behind the Beatles.

45

The Searchers. From left to right: John McNally, Frank Allen, Chris Curtis, Mike Pender.

OPPOSITE: The Moody Blues. Clockwise from top left: Ray Thomas, Mike Pinder, Denny Laine, Graeme Edge, Clint Warwick.

Brian Poole and the Tremeloes, the first southern band to break through during the beat boom, reaching #1 with a cover of the Contours' 'Do You Love Me'.

The format that was devised was simple: every show would end with the week's #1 single, no record would be played two weeks in succession unless it was at #1, and no record would feature if it was dropping down the charts. From the outset, therefore, the interest was in reflecting popular taste, as shown in the chart positions, rather than in showcasing the best acts available or trying to set the agenda for pop music. Having repeatedly failed to keep pace with the appetite for rock and roll, it seemed as though the BBC had simply abandoned the attempt and decided to let the public make its own way. To some extent this followed on from the already established *Juke Box Jury*, where a panel of celebrities, some of them associated with music, reviewed new records simply in terms of whether they would be hits or misses. Like that show, *Top of the Pops* mirrored the slavish devotion to weekly sales figures that – uniquely in the cultural world – lay at the heart of the pop industry. Why this should have been so was never entirely clear, but the convention was by now firmly entrenched, to the extent that in March 1964 even the *Daily Telegraph* began to print the week's top ten.

Jack Good, who had invented pop television in Britain with *Six-Five Special* and *Oh Boy!* in the 1950s, was unimpressed by the restrictions of the series: 'If you want to see who's in the top twenty this week you turn on *Top of the Pops* in the same way you'd look at the news or weather forecast,' he commented. 'It's really become non-fiction. My stuff was fiction.' In the early days, when bands were allowed to mime to their records – 'a departure from normal BBC practice', noted the *Radio Times* – the literalness of the show's format was even more notable: the camera showed Denise Sampey (later replaced by Samantha Juste) putting a record on the turntable, closed in on the needle dropping into the groove and then dissolved into the act on stage as they mimed to the music. Meanwhile the audience danced in the background, responsible and respectful in their enthusiasm: 'P.J. Proby gets pawed by teenagers on *Ready Steady Go!* where it's usual,' noted one critic, 'and politely left alone on *Top of the Pops*, where it's not.'

When it became apparent that the series was going to continue beyond its initial six-week run, Savile decided against remaining as the sole host and took his place in a rotating team of presenters, alongside BBC stalwarts Pete Murray, David Jacobs and Alan Freeman, a roster that remained in place for the first three years. Again the conservatism of the BBC could hardly fail to be noticed: the average age of the four presenters at the start of the series was 37, while that of the singers on the first episode was just 21. *Ready Steady Go!*, by contrast, had made a star of 21-year-old Cathy McGowan, chosen to present because she represented the viewing public: gawky, hesitant and quite frequently star-struck.

What *Top of the Pops* did have in its favour, however, was the personality of Savile himself. Relentlessly extrovert and dedicated to self-promotion, he had pioneered the use of twin turntables when working as a DJ after the war, and had become a cult figure in the Manchester clubs at the turn of the 1960s before moving into radio. With his long hair dyed in a succession of unexpected colours (despite this being the era of black-and-white television), his wardrobe that owed nothing to taste and his vocal delivery that consisted mostly of wrongly stressed words and semi-yodels, he was unlike anything seen before on television. He was, wrote critic George Melly, 'fascinatingly dreadful', but he was hard to ignore. 'That man is box office,' said Johnnie Stewart; 'a kind of 20th-century clown.'

His contribution came not simply in front of the cameras, but in creating the atmosphere backstage. 'The crew were tripping over each other. It was ramshackle, like people were making it up as they went along,' remembered Keith Richards of his appearance on the first edition with the Rolling Stones.

Two more southern rivals to the northern beat groups: Dave Clark (below) and Dave Dee (bottom); Clark was later to buy the rights to the *Ready Steady Go!* archive.

The top twenty in June 1965
on *Top of the Pops*.

'Jimmy Savile's energy kept it all together.' Already a star, he turned the show into a success, and it is unlikely that it would have made the same immediate impact without him. In 1965 readers of the *New Musical Express* in their annual poll placed *Top of the Pops* as the best television show of the year, replacing *Ready Steady Go!*, the first of seven successive victories; Savile had already been voted best disc jockey and was to remain in top place right up to 1971.

Somehow the simplicity of the format struck a chord. Within a matter of months the programme was regularly finding itself in the television top twenty and becoming essential viewing for the nation's teenagers. For some, it was a communal experience: 'I remember screaming at the television screen, along with my friends,' one fan was later to recall. 'We'd be into a chorus of screams until someone stuck their head round the door and said, "Shut up, for goodness sake."' For others it was part of the family routine, even when parents disapproved of what they saw. 'My mother watched the Stones on *Top of the Pops* and fretted about the unhygienic nature of their hair,' wrote comedian Griff Rhys Jones. 'And', he admitted, 'at thirteen we rather agreed with her. They were too noisy and had aggressive lips.'

By the time Huw Wheldon became the managing director of BBC television in 1968, he found that the show, now fixed in its familiar slot of 7.30 pm on Thursdays, was the only early-evening ratings winner capable of delivering a majority audience for the Corporation against ITV competition.

For the stars too, it had become a regular fixture and one of the most coveted of gigs. 'We loved doing *Top of the Pops* because it meant we were probably going to encounter the Rolling Stones or the Supremes or Roy Orbison,' enthused Peter Noone. 'It was an incredible chance to meet your heroes.' And, as some of the early fans themselves became musicians, so an invitation to appear was increasingly seen as a mark of success, investing the show with a mythology and status that no other British pop programme was ever to achieve. Rick Parfitt of Status Quo, the band who played more often on the series than any other act, made his debut in early 1968: 'Like everybody else in Britain of my generation, I watched it avidly as a fan, so the thought of actually being on there at last with my own group – it was unimaginable, dream-laden stuff.'

TONIGHT'S TOP 20

1	LONG LIVE LOVE	Sandie Shaw	
2	A WORLD OF OUR OWN	The Seekers	
3	THE CLAPPING SONG	Shirley Ellis	
4	POOR MAN'S SON	The Rockin' Berries	
5	WHERE ARE YOU NOW	Jackie Trent	
6	TRAINS & BOATS & PLANES	Burt Bacharach	
6	THE PRICE OF LOVE	Everly Brothers	
8	TRUE LOVE WAYS	Peter & Gordon	
9	CRYING IN THE CHAPEL	Elvis Presley	
10	THIS LITTLE BIRD	Marianne Faithfull	
11	KING OF THE ROAD	Roger Miller	
12	MARIE	The Bachelors	
13	TICKET TO RIDE	The Beatles	
14	SUBTERRANEAN HOMESICK BLUES	Bob Dylan	
15	NOT UNTIL THE NEXT TIME	Jim Reeves	
	TRAINS & BOATS & PLANES	Billy J. Kramer / Dakotas	
		The Hollies	Françoise Hardy

chapter two

YEH YEH

The record industry, which had been so conspicuously slow to recognize developments in the clubs of the Midlands and the North, went on to repeat the error in London itself. Under the leadership of Cyril Davies and Alexis Korner, a splinter of the 1950s jazz scene had taken to playing electric rhythm and blues, inspired by the amplified blues of American artists such as Muddy Waters and Jimmy Reed, and by 1962 had begun to establish itself at clubs including the Marquee, the Crawdaddy and the Flamingo. The impact on the audiences was as powerful as it had been at the Downbeat in Newcastle or at the Cavern in Liverpool: 'Everything was special,' remembered future pop star David Essex of his first visit to the Flamingo as a young teenager. 'The records the club played. The energy of the place. I felt like I had discovered the meaning of life.' He promptly abandoned his football ambitions (he was on the books of West Ham as a schoolboy) and bought a drum kit, so that he too could become a musician.

In the rush to sign up groups who sounded as much like the Beatles as possible, however, the record companies paid no heed to this circuit, preferring instead Brian Poole and the Tremeloes, who came from Essex but could pass for Merseybeat in a poor light. It was only when the Rolling Stones broke into the top twenty in December 1963, with a Lennon-McCartney song, 'I Wanna Be Your Man', as performed on the first edition of *Top of the Pops*, that attitudes changed, and the familiar race to sign every London R&B act began in earnest.

In the meantime an entire subculture had appeared that should have suggested that something was happening amongst the capital's youth, and that there might be a musical dimension worth exploiting. Initially, however, the rise of mod culture was primarily a fashion phenomenon, deriving from the taste amongst modernist jazz fans for continental style. More specifically, it was a

OPPOSITE: The Beatles.

The Beatles at the
Manchester Apollo.

OPPOSITE: The Rolling Stones in the *Top of the Pops* studio.

male fashion phenomenon: 'One didn't only dress up for girls,' reflected the hero of Gillian Freeman's 1961 novel *The Leather Boys*. 'One didn't only have clean shoes and a brushed suit because one wanted girls to admire one. His appearance mattered to himself. The time he spent on it was entirely for his own satisfaction. Well, perhaps not entirely. Some was for the other boys, in peacock competition.'

It wasn't just in fiction that peer approval became more important than courtship rituals: 'Girls were out of fashion, almost, and the guys wore the suits to impress the other guys,' commented one mod. 'It was almost as if the roles had been reversed. The boys were getting prettier and the girls were getting plainer.' Pete Townshend, who became a mod hero with the Who, had a similar recollection: 'The whole mod thing was a blending of sexes, the girls looked like boys and the boys looked a bit like girls: even though they wore suits, they wore make-up.' In short, as George Melly was to point out: 'They were true dandies, interested in creating works of art – themselves. There had of course been dandies before but they'd always been upper-class dandies. Now Macmillan's affluence had helped create working-class dandies.'

BELOW LEFT: The Rolling Stones.

BELOW RIGHT: The Rolling Stones in the canteen at the BBC studios in Dickenson Road, Manchester.

ABOVE AND OPPOSITE: The Rolling Stones. Clockwise from top left: Bill Wyman, Brian Jones, Keith Richards, Charlie Watts and (opposite) Mick Jagger.

Georgie Fame and (left) his band, the Blue Flames.

The class issue was important. Mod evolved in the East End of London and in Shepherd's Bush amongst working-class youths who found themselves in a position where employment was relatively easy to find, certainly compared with their parents' experience, and who were determined to stake their claim in an upwardly mobile society, preferably in the most conspicuous manner possible. The means to this end was fashion, following Mark Twain's dictum that clothes make the man, and for some at least, this was not simply a youth cult but a new attitude to life: 'We hope to stay smart for ever,' commented one, 'not shoddy like our parents.'

The heart of the action was Carnaby Street, which had become increasingly associated with boutiques since John Stephen opened the shop His Clothes there in 1959 (at one point Stephen had eight shops on the street). By April 1966, when a celebrated *Time* magazine cover story anointed London as the city of the decade – 'It swings; it is the scene' – Carnaby Street had become a tourist attraction for the world, to such an extent that a police officer was put on duty to keep the crowds moving so that everyone might exercise their democratic right to window-shop. But by then it was long past its peak; the Kinks had already mocked the 'Dedicated Follower of Fashion', and as early as summer 1964 there were those who knew that the glory years had passed: 'There's quite a crisis in the real mod world about all these fashions and dances leaking out so quickly,' regretted one trendsetter. 'The pace of change has been hotted up so much – a clothes fashion and a dance fashion could last for about three months before, but now they're being imitated by all these little "Chods" from the countryside.'

The Kinks. From left to right: Mick Avory, Peter Quaife, Dave Davies, Ray Davies.

The key to this 'turnover-worship', as journalist Bernard Levin described it, was television and in particular Rediffusion's series for ITV, *Ready Steady Go!* First broadcast in August 1963, *RSG!* was to become for three crucial years one

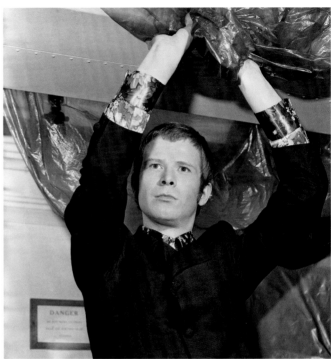

Two of the best vocalists on the London R&B club circuit: Chris Farlowe (left) and Long John Baldry (right).

of the most important media for shaping youth culture in the country, though producer Vicki Wickham saw it as being essentially reflective: 'It wasn't some great idea we had – it was the '60s on the screen. Young people in the mod fashion of the day dancing the dances that young people were learning from America to music that was being influenced by America.' Despite her protestations, the show had an approach and an attitude that was unusual on British television. Like *Oh Boy!* in the 1950s, *RSG!* came with an agenda: it booked acts on style rather than sales (the Rolling Stones appeared in the third episode because Wickham thought Brian Jones 'was the most gorgeous chap we'd ever seen'); it employed a designer, Nicholas Ferguson, recruited from the Slade art school, who fed off the latest innovations of Pop Art; and – as the series progressed – it recruited its studio audience from the best dancers at the Scene Club. This was the in crowd of London being transmitted nationwide: 'A mod programme which the groups and the audience very nearly turned into a piece of street theatre,' wrote Alan Fletcher in his novelization of the Who's 1979 film *Quadrophenia*, set in 1964. 'A programme which unified the whole movement across the country, transmitting its music and advertising its fashions.'

At the show's heart was Cathy McGowan, who presented alongside the more staid Radio Luxembourg disc jockey Keith Fordyce, and whose fluffs and

OPPOSITE: Manfred Mann. Clockwise from left: Manfred Mann, Paul Jones, Mike Hugg, Tom McGuinness.

tongue-tied miscues bridged the gap between audience and stars. 'She was awfully gauche and raw and desperately nervous,' said co-creator Elkan Allan, 'but she was worth taking on because she was obviously terribly switched on in a teenage way.' Her position as an arbiter of taste reflected that of the show itself: '*Ready Steady Go!* was the showcase,' said John McConnell, who worked as a graphic designer with the boutique Biba; 'dress Cathy McGowan on Friday, and on Saturday there was a queue round the block.' Looked up to as a fashion icon, McGowan didn't lose sight of the fact that it was male style that really counted in this world: 'For girls, looking deliberately dowdy is the thing,' she opined, 'dull colours and old ladies' shoes, although girls are more attractive if they've got a really marvellous, way-out pair of boots. It's the boys who have to look pretty with red and pink trousers and high-heeled boots.'

The Small Faces. Clockwise from left: Ronnie Lane, Steve Marriott, Ian MacLagan, Kenny Jones.

Similarly, if less obviously, Ferguson's set designs brought contemporary art to an entirely new audience and helped shape the taste of an increasingly design-literate country. And, of course, in musical terms it was hugely influential. Like the teds of the early 1950s, mods had started with fashion but had then embraced music, before departing from the pattern and producing their own groups. This music became the bedrock for *RSG!*, which broke new acts, from the Who to Marc Bolan, and provided a national platform for visiting legends from America, including John Lee Hooker and Rufus Thomas. There were, however, limits to the power of the programme. In March 1965 it brought a Tamla Motown special to

OPPOSITE: The Who. From left to right: Roger Daltrey, John Entwhistle, Keith Moon, Pete Townshend.

the screen, at a time when, despite cover versions by the Beatles, Rolling Stones and many others, the Supremes were the only act on the label scoring big hits in their own right in Britain; they featured in the show, alongside the Miracles, the Temptations, Stevie Wonder and Martha and the Vandellas. A package tour followed, but outside London and Manchester the gigs were a disastrous flop, and Motown achieved just one top twenty hit in Britain that year.

Despite such occasional failures, *RSG!* was the show that staged London's fight back against the northern beat boom. The summer of 1964 saw #1 hits for a trio of the capital's leading bands, the Rolling Stones, Manfred Mann and the Kinks, with the Yardbirds, Georgie Fame and the Blue Flames, and the Who following hot on their heels. Few of the hit singles were R&B as would have been

Keith Moon (left), Roger Daltrey (centre) and Pete Townshend (right). 'The mod look was very clean-cut, Ivy League, fashion conscious,' remembered Roger Daltrey, 'which was exactly opposite from the Stones.'

heard on the club circuit just a year earlier – Fame, for example, renowned for the intensity of his Hammond-driven live act at the Flamingo Club, scored with the much lighter 'Yeh Yeh', while the Yardbirds' guitarist, Eric Clapton, was so disenchanted with the pop sound of their first big hit, 'For Your Love', that he promptly left the band. But even allowing for the compromises made in the name of commercialism, the groups collectively favoured a much tougher, more swaggering approach to music than Merseybeat had achieved. In so doing, they followed in the mod convention and opened a gender divide, as Roger Daltrey, lead singer of the Who, acknowledged: 'Before us, groups were popular first with girls. The Who was more popular with men, basically because we were so aggressive.'

They also brought an overt aesthetic sensibility to rock and roll for the first time. 'The British are not an artistic race,' mocked the writer Quentin Crisp: 'they go to art schools not to acquire skills in the arts but to avoid real life for a few adolescent years.' Nonetheless former art school students like Pete Townshend, Keith Richards and Kinks frontman Ray Davies acquired a level of sophistication and self-conscious creativity that had previously been unknown in British pop: when the Who smashed their instruments up on stage, Townshend was quick to link it to the auto-destructive art advocated by Gustav Metzger, a visiting lecturer at his college. 'Pop Art borrowed from real pop,' he explained in 1966, 'and we're taking it back again.' Others were making the same connexions. Magazine designer Pearce Marchbank remembered going to an exhibition in 1964 'which had a whole room full of American Pop Art: Rauschenberg, Jasper Johns, targets and flags and what have you. Then you'd drift off to see the Who and you'd put two and two together. There seemed to be a direct line between what was on at the Tate Gallery and what was on at the Marquee.' David Hockney made a collage of newspaper and magazine articles about the Rolling Stones, and Andy Warhol himself was to pay tribute, going backstage at a New York gig because 'I wanted to be in the presence of the Yardbirds.'

The Righteous Brothers, whose records were produced by Phil Spector.

Two of the most celebrated girl groups of the 1960s, the Ronettes (opposite) and the Supremes (above).

OPPOSITE: Lee Dorsey, whose hits 'Working in the Coalmine' and 'Holy Cow' made him a star in Britain.

LEFT AND BELOW: James Brown, who never replicated his American chart successes in Britain, but was hugely influential.

OPPOSITE: Multi-instrumentalist
Stevie Wonder.

There was also the social scene of London, with the rise of late-night
discotheques such as the Ad Lib, the Scotch of St James and the Cromwellian,
which provided the sense of being part of the most fashionable society in the
world. It was 'a wonderful scene', said Dave Clark. 'It was a cultural revolution
in music, fashion, art, theatre, movies, and we were all one – you'd go to a
restaurant and there would be Princess Margaret, Michael Caine, Sean Connery,
Terence Stamp, the Stones and Beatles, and all the
writers and directors.'

Dave Berry, whose pop
hits seldom reflected the
charismatic power of his
live performances.

Amongst the few Merseybeat groups who fitted
into this world of art and celebrity were the Beatles,
partly because they were the biggest stars of them all,
and partly because they had themselves come from
similar backgrounds to their London counterparts,
Lennon in particular having attended the Liverpool
College of Art. 'When we came down to London, all
we did was plug out of the Liverpool student scene and
plug into the London student scene,' remembered Paul
McCartney. 'Like, up north you'd be reading *On the
Road* and they would be reading *On the Road*. We'd
be looking at the same kind of things.'

They also shared a determination not to get
sucked into the light entertainment circuit that had
trapped previous British rock stars, from Lonnie
Donegan to Adam Faith: this time round it would be
left to Gerry and the Pacemakers and Freddie and the
Dreamers to make their way into pantomime.
'England has such a small show business community
that if you don't become part of it and join the Variety
Club and do charity work, then you're looked upon as
some kind of weirdo,' shuddered Mick Jagger in retrospect. 'I tried not to be part
of it.' In 1963 the Beatles had appeared on the family entertainment shows *The
Morecambe and Wise Show* and *Big Night Out* with Mike and Bernie Winters, but
by 1965 John Lennon was turning up on Peter Cook and Dudley Moore's *Not Only
… But Also*, a much hipper comedy vehicle altogether. The previous year he had
published his first book, a collection of stories, poems and nonsense titled *In His
Own Write*, and had been at pains to point out that this wasn't what a pop star
normally did: 'He learns to tap-dance. We don't want to learn to dance or take

elocution lessons.' There was a solidarity between the groups, a mutual support system, as Jagger acknowledged: 'In a small society the pressures to conform are immense, but in a big city like this, and especially when you're mixing with people who don't care, it's very easy to do exactly as you like.'

As the interaction between the musicians developed, so it became apparent that there was a thin line between community and rivalry. The Beatles' second album, *With the Beatles* (1963), came in the best dressed sleeve thus far in British pop music, a stylish black-and-white photograph by Robert Freeman of the band wearing polo-neck jumpers, their side-lit faces hovering in the blackness. In response, the Stones' debut album, *The Rolling Stones* (1964), featured a similarly atmospheric photo by David Bailey, but with no identifying information at all, whether of band or album title – they looked so cool that any prospective purchaser worth his salt was evidently supposed to know who they were. In later years, the Beatles were to enlist the two biggest hitters of the British Pop Art world, Peter Blake and Richard Hamilton, to design the covers for *Sgt Pepper's Lonely Hearts Club Band* (1967) and *The Beatles* (1968) respectively, seeming to raise the bar impossibly high, until the Stones enlisted Andy Warhol for the sleeve of *Sticky Fingers* (1971).

Musically, too, the interplay of influence saw the songwriting of Lennon and McCartney become the measure by which other groups were judged, even while the Beatles were cheerfully appropriating the use of feedback, as pioneered by the Yardbirds and the Kinks, on 'I Feel Fine'. In terms of direct sales competition, however, there was considerably more caution displayed, at least in relation to the two biggest bands; the first Stones record to reach #1 was 'It's All Over Now', which spent just one week at the top in July 1964 before being replaced by the Beatles' 'A Hard Day's Night' – thereafter, there was to be no clash in release dates for singles by the two groups.

The film that accompanied that Beatles single was perhaps the most significant statement of intent the band had yet delivered. Previous movies with rock and roll stars had seldom amounted to more than an excuse to put a handful of mimed songs on screen, with the few exceptions (*King Creole, Expresso Bongo, Beat Girl*) all notable for having not been conceived specifically for the singers who appeared in them. *A Hard Day's Night* (1964), directed by Richard Lester, offered a new direction: it was the first film that seemed to be part of rock and roll, rather than an outsider's view. The Beatles played themselves, or simplified versions thereof, in a variety of settings that reflected the chaos of their lives; lost in long periods of boredom, punctuated by the completion of contractual obligations, they looked trapped by their success, with only a gang mentality to

Dusty Springfield, 'the Judy Garland of the "in" set', as George Melly called her.

fall back on as defence against the demands of managers, television producers and public. It was cheerfully cynical about the manipulations of the media industry and about stardom itself, it avoided the rags-to-riches and the let's-put-the-show-on-right-here clichés of earlier films and it further distanced the band from the world of light entertainment.

The film should have inaugurated a wave of genuinely good rock movies, but when the Rolling Stones failed to realize their aspirations to film either Anthony Burgess's novel *A Clockwork Orange* (1962) or, their second choice, *Only Lovers Left Alive* (1964) by Dave Wallis, it was left to the Dave Clark Five to make the only worthy successor. *Catch Us if You Can* (1965) was a surprisingly sullen piece ('as if Pop Art had discovered Chekhov', claimed critic Pauline Kael) that unusually didn't cast the band as musicians, and in which Clark didn't even get the girl at the end. It continued the knowingness of the Beatles – 'that's her image,' shrugs an advertising executive of a young actress employed to promote

Dusty Springfield, backstage and (right) on *Top of the Pops*.

meat, 'rootless, classless, product of affluence, typical of modern youth' – and threw in middle-class decadence, proto-hippies and heroin references as a bonus.

Despite the lack of comparable follow-ups, including the Beatles' own next film, *Help!* (1965), which failed to repeat the critical success, *A Hard Day's Night* emphasized that, for the first time in British rock, musicians were setting their own agenda, retaining their hip status despite all attempts to co-opt them.

The most entertaining of those attempts came in June 1965 when the four members of the group were each awarded an MBE by Harold Wilson, prompting a wave of outrage and of honours being returned in protest by previous recipients; a former RAF squadron leader who sent back his MBE summed up the mood: 'I feel that when people like the Beatles are given the MBE the whole thing becomes debased and cheapened.' Cabinet minister Barbara Castle recorded that Labour MPs were unimpressed ('The reaction was wholly unfavourable, the word "gimmick" being prominent'), and the artistic establishment was no less displeased, with Noel Coward noting: 'Some other decoration should have been selected to reward them for their talentless but considerable contribution to the exchequer.' Meanwhile the Downing Street mailbag revealed that disapproving letters outnumbered those in support by a ratio of two to one, though since a good many were from fans of other bands that had somehow been overlooked, that fact wasn't perhaps overly significant.

Given that the same honours list awarded OBEs to singer Frankie Vaughan and to television actor Jack Warner of *Dixon of Dock Green* fame, it wasn't entirely clear what the fuss was about. Certainly the Beatles were younger than most recipients, but then their foreign earnings – which had been what prompted the award – were considerably greater. A more serious concern was that put by another cabinet minister, Anthony Wedgwood Benn: 'The plain truth is that the Beatles have done more for the royal family by accepting MBEs than the royal family have done for the Beatles by giving them,' he wrote in his diary. 'Nobody goes to see the Beatles because they've got MBEs but the royal family love the idea that the honours list is popular because it all helps to buttress them, and indirectly their influence is used to strengthen all the forces of conservatism in society.' He needn't have worried: the award did little to make the establishment fashionable. If anything the danger was in the other direction, a fear expressed by Elkan Allan, co-creator of *Ready Steady Go!*: 'When the Beatles got the MBE, pop music just became too respectable.' The playwright Joe Orton, commissioned to write a screenplay for a Beatles film that sadly never happened, made the same point, albeit obliquely, to Paul McCartney: 'The theatre started going downhill when Queen Victoria knighted Henry Irving. Too fucking respectable.'

The Zombies. From left to right: Colin Blunstone, Paul Atkinson, Rod Argent, Hugh Grundy, Chris White.

But even those fears didn't really materialize. The Beatles managed to carry off the MBEs episode without seeming to have made any concessions to the establishment, and subsequently claimed that they'd smoked a joint in the lavatories while waiting. Wilson himself was to comment in later years that: 'They were regarded as clean-living lads during the time they were getting established, whatever may have gone on later.' Which suggested that perhaps he wasn't quite as in touch as he liked to appear.

In any event, fans of bad behaviour could always count on the Rolling Stones. The month after the Beatles' awards were announced, the *Daily Mirror* reported an incident when the Stones pulled into a petrol station and were refused permission to use the lavatory, with a mechanic asking them to leave. Mick Jagger 'brushed him aside, saying, "We will piss anywhere, man." This was taken up by the group as a chant as one of them danced. Wyman, Jagger and Jones were seen to urinate on a wall of the garage. The car drove off with people inside sticking their hands through the windows in a well-known gesture.' The three offenders were fined five pounds each for insulting behaviour.

OPPOSITE: The Ivy League, whose John Carter and Ken Lewis went on to create the Flower Pot Men and to record 'We Love the Pirates' under the name the Roaring Sixties.

chapter three

CATCH THE WIND

In the great rush of English bands in 1963 and 1964, it seemed almost as though American records were becoming an endangered species in the British charts. Old favourites like Elvis Presley and the Everly Brothers continued to score hits, though seldom reaching the top ten any more, and a few new names made an impression: the Supremes, the Four Seasons and Gene Pitney (the latter boosted by his association with the Rolling Stones, covering Jagger and Richards' 'That Girl Belongs to Yesterday'). But these were the exceptions rather than the rule, as was Chuck Berry, who finally became a major chart star in Britain, in the wake of his songs being covered by the Beatles and others. Beyond the charts, however, there was one figure whose presence could not long be ignored.

Bob Dylan, a rock and roll fan who had taken to singing folk music in the clubs of New York, released his eponymous first album in 1962 and visited Britain in the winter of the same year, primarily to appear in a BBC television play, *Madhouse on Castle Street*. The album sold poorly, as initially did its successor, *The Freewheelin' Bob Dylan* in 1963 (though that did eventually reach #1 two years after its release), but amongst those few who heard the records, the impact was considerable, and his became a fashionable name to drop in the right circles. Whether on traditional songs or performing his own compositions, he had the aura and authority of a prophet who sounded as though he'd been born old, singing with what David Bowie was later to describe as 'a voice like sand and glue'.

For the pop market, Dylan first registered as the composer of 'Blowin' in the Wind', a 1963 hit for folk-pop trio Peter, Paul and Mary both in America, where it was followed into the charts by their cover of 'Don't Think Twice, It's Alright', and in Britain, where it was followed by nothing. His real breakthrough came the following year when the Animals covered on consecutive singles two songs that

OPPOSITE: Bob Dylan.

Jonathan King, whose first hit, 'Everyone's Gone to the Moon', parodied the protest boom.

OPPOSITE: The Byrds. From left to right: Michael Clarke, Gene Clark, Roger McGuinn, David Crosby, Chris Hillman.

their producer, Mickie Most, had found on Dylan's debut album: 'Baby Let Me Take You Home' stopped just shy of the top twenty, but 'House of the Rising Sun' went to #1 in Britain and America and was to become one of the most influential records of the decade.

The ubiquity of the Beatles hadn't gone unnoticed on the American folk scene, and there were some, including Dylan himself, who were impressed not only by the success but by the quality of their music. 'They were doing things nobody else was doing. Their chords were outrageous, just outrageous, and their harmonies made it all valid,' he commented later. 'But I just kept it to myself that I really dug them. Everybody else thought they were for the teenyboppers.' Despite the early interest, it was far from clear how folk and British beat could be reconciled, until the Animals' 'House of the Rising Sun', a powerful, electric rock treatment of a traditional song, complete with barnstorming vocals, showed the way forward. Dylan was enthused ('It's fucking *wild!* Blew my mind'), and within months he had left behind his established instrumentation of acoustic guitar and harmonica and was being backed by a full electric band.

Also in 1964, a series of hits by Merseybeat band the Searchers gave another suggestion for the future. 'Needles and Pins' featured close vocal harmonies and a ringing guitar sound that became the group's signature, replicated on stage and on sequels – 'When You Walk in the Room' and 'What Have They Done to the Rain' – with the use of an electric 12-string guitar. The newly formed American group, the Byrds, were to adapt that sound for their cover of the Dylan song 'Mr Tambourine Man' to create what would become known as folk-rock, the chart sensation of 1965 and the first major response to the British invasion. The Byrds were hailed as America's answer to the Beatles and, although a British tour in support of their second hit, another Dylan song 'All I Really Want to Do', failed to convince the public (some shows were cancelled owing to lack of sales, and subsequent singles missed the top twenty), their influence was soon to be discerned even in the work of the Beatles themselves.

In Britain the moment that folk-rock came together was March 1965 when Donovan, a young Scottish musician, appeared on *Ready Steady Go!* to sing his first single, 'Catch the Wind', a slightly dippy acoustic song, unavoidably reminiscent of Dylan; a fortnight later it was entering the charts, in the same week that Dylan made his own debut with 'The Times They Are a-Changin''. In their wake came hits that year not just for the Byrds, but also Joan Baez and Sonny and Cher, the latter duo riding the folk-rock wave with the #1 single 'I Got You, Babe', a perfect piece of pop that was essentially a return to the high school sounds of pre-Beatles days, even if it were draped in all the fashionable accoutrements.

At the centre of it all was Dylan, reaching a creative peak – both for himself and for rock and roll – with the six-minute single, 'Like a Rolling Stone', which was aimed directly at the pop market. Reborn now, having jettisoned his folkie image along with the music, he looked like a speed-driven cross between beatnik and mod, and was taking the Beatles' mockery of interviewers and the industry to new heights: 'I don't want to be interviewed by your paper,' he told *Disc* magazine. 'I don't need it. You don't need it either. You can build up your own star. Why don't you just get a lot of money and bring some kid out here from

OPPOSITE: Donovan, whose hits included a cover of 'Universal Soldier' from the debut album by Buffy Sainte-Marie (below right).

BELOW LEFT: Sonny and Cher, who became international stars in the folk-rock era.

BELOW RIGHT: Buffy Sainte-Marie.

The Beach Boys. From
left to right: Al Jardine,
Brian Wilson, Carl Wilson,
Dennis Wilson, Mike Love.

the north of England and say: "We're gonna make you a star. You just comply
with everything we do."' His influence on the songwriting of British groups was
apparent on the Beatles' single 'Help!' and on the Rolling Stones' '(I Can't Get
No) Satisfaction', both #1 hits in 1965, the former introducing a much more
personal and downbeat note to their lyrics and the latter featuring Mick Jagger's
elliptical lyrics about the frustrations of modern life.

Falling even more directly under Dylan's shadow were Manfred Mann, who
covered his song 'With God on Our Side' on their EP *The One in the Middle*,
released in June 1965. Banned by the BBC, who considered its anti-war lyrics too
political, the song was performed by the group on *Ready Steady Go!* and sparked
a brief boom in protest songs, including Barry McGuire's imported 'Eve of
Destruction' (also banned by the BBC), as well as home-grown records ranging
from Donovan's cover of Buffy Sainte-Marie's 'Universal Solider' to Jonathan
King's 'Everyone's Gone to the Moon', written as a send-up of what he considered
the pretensions of protest, and King's composition 'It's Good News Week', a hit
for Hedgehoppers Anonymous. The industry's attitude to this new development
was summed up by the manager of the Hollies, when they released 'Too Many
People', a song about over-population: 'I suppose it will be controversial, but that
never did any harm. It's publicity, and with a record you're just selling product.'
His cynicism was misplaced: the song and its A-side 'Very Last Day' proved to
be the band's first flop single after nine consecutive top twenty hits.

The best of these protest songs were fine pop records, which was fortunate,
for they amounted to very little as political statements. In America, where male
teenagers faced the prospect of being drafted for Vietnam, even the simplest
declaration against war had a resonance, though the GIs themselves seemed to
prefer something with a harder edge: a 1967 *New York Times* article headlined
ROCK 'N' ROLL SONG BECOMING VIETNAM'S TIPPERARY reported that American
soldiers in South-East Asia had adopted as an anthem the Animals' 'We Gotta
Get Out of This Place' (another record from the protest summer of 1965). In
Britain, however, no such threat hung over the heads of the nation's youth, and
there was no popular political movement to which protest songs could relate; the
Campaign for Nuclear Disarmament might have filled the role, but that had been
primarily associated with the trad jazz movement and had been outflanked when
the three existing nuclear powers signed the first Test Ban Treaty in 1963. It had
also foundered on its own frustrations and failure – as Pete Townshend, who had
been on the Aldermaston marches as a schoolboy, pointed out: 'we achieved
nothing and felt we achieved nothing.' By the time of the protest boom, it had

OPPOSITE: Paul Simon and Art Garfunkel, the next generation of folk-rock.

Zalman Yanovsky, guitarist in the New York band the Lovin' Spoonful.

faded almost entirely away, leaving behind little but the Cheshire cat grin of the CND badge sported by Paul Jones of Manfred Mann.

In reality there wasn't a great deal to protest about for British pop. National Service had ended, Britain was politely declining America's invitations to get involved in Vietnam and, while Harold Wilson's government might have been struggling with the economy and with rising union militancy, these have seldom been the concern of rock and roll. The issues that had a more straightforward appeal were all being addressed, and were to be resolved, in the interests of liberalism: a raft of legislation in the late 1960s saw the legalization of abortion and of male homosexuality, the ending of capital punishment and of censorship of the stage and literature, and the restraint of racism. These later advances were on the agenda by 1965, and in any event there were some things for young people to celebrate more immediately: this was the year that Boots, the country's largest chain of chemists, decided for the first time to stock condoms, removing the need to hope that a trip to the barber would end with the words: 'Something for the weekend, sir?'

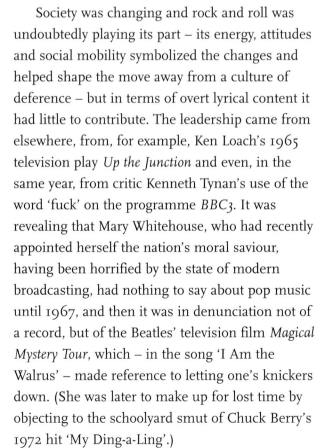

Society was changing and rock and roll was undoubtedly playing its part – its energy, attitudes and social mobility symbolized the changes and helped shape the move away from a culture of deference – but in terms of overt lyrical content it had little to contribute. The leadership came from elsewhere, from, for example, Ken Loach's 1965 television play *Up the Junction* and even, in the same year, from critic Kenneth Tynan's use of the word 'fuck' on the programme *BBC3*. It was revealing that Mary Whitehouse, who had recently appointed herself the nation's moral saviour, having been horrified by the state of modern broadcasting, had nothing to say about pop music until 1967, and then it was in denunciation not of a record, but of the Beatles' television film *Magical Mystery Tour*, which – in the song 'I Am the Walrus' – made reference to letting one's knickers down. (She was later to make up for lost time by objecting to the schoolyard smut of Chuck Berry's 1972 hit 'My Ding-a-Ling'.)

RIGHT: Françoise Hardy, whose biggest British hit was the English-language 'All Over the World'.

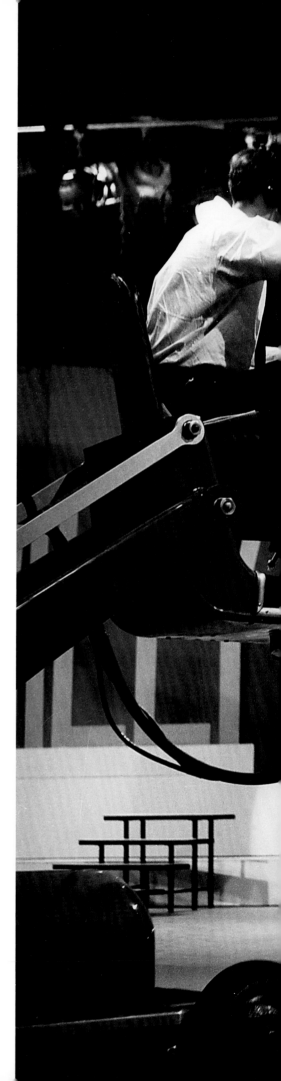

RIGHT: Françoise Hardy, whose biggest British hit was the English-language 'All Over the World'.

What the protest boom did achieve, however, was a broadening of the range of lyrical concerns now considered acceptable in rock and roll, even if much of the running was to be made, paradoxically, by one of the few leading British bands not to fall under the spell of Dylan. In September 1965 the Kinks released an EP *Kwyet Kinks* that contained the song 'Well Respected Man', a satirical attack on the upper classes, and followed it the next year with a trio of hits that addressed unusual issues for pop songs and did so with humour rather than solemnity: 'Dedicated Follower of Fashion', 'Sunny Afternoon' and 'Dead End Street'. Others followed in 1966, including the Who ('I'm a Boy') and the Rolling Stones ('Mother's Little Helper'). The position of 'Taxman' by the Beatles was less clear – it dealt with high levels of taxation under the Labour government, as did 'Sunny Afternoon', but it was perhaps more accurately regarded as a protest song on behalf of the extremely wealthy.

Jackie Trent, who had a #1 hit with 'Where Are You Now (My Love)', co-written with her future husband, Tony Hatch.

Marianne Faithfull (left) and Nancy Sinatra (right), whose first hits benefitted from collaborations with Mick Jagger and Keith Richards, and Lee Hazlewood respectively.

OPPOSITE: Petula Clark, Britain's most successful female singer ever.

The music coming from America in 1966 was likewise changing. Folk-rock continued to produce new stars in the shape of Simon and Garfunkel, the Lovin' Spoonful and the Mamas and the Papas, but their records were lighter, less portentous, even downright happy by comparison with, say, 'Eve of Destruction'. Dylan contributed his most jokey song, 'Rainy Day Women #12 & 35', and the mood of the year seemed encapsulated in the fact that the Beach Boys enjoyed a protracted run of success in Britain for the first time, with a string of four top ten singles that culminated in 'Good Vibrations'. Or perhaps the times were summed up by the top two singles in the last British chart of the year: at #2 was 'Sunshine Superman', Donovan's first excursion into fully electric music, under the guidance of Mickie Most, while at #1 (as it had been all month) was the sentimental country melodrama of Tom Jones' 'Green Green Grass of Home'.

The success of Jones' record was significant, for running alongside the folk-rock and protest era had been a resurgence in the popularity of middle-of-the-road ballads. The two were not entirely separate, for there were certain points of contact: in the non-rock instrumentation that accompanied the early hits of Marianne Faithfull, perhaps, or in the folk-based easy-listening pop of Australian band the Seekers, who had the biggest selling single of 1965 in Britain with 'I'll Never Find Another You'.

More significant than either, however, was Petula Clark, whose re-emergence in the 1960s took a somewhat circuitous route. A former child actress (she had appeared with the legendary comedian Sid Field in the 1946 film *London Town*), she had been a successful singer in the mid 1950s, both on television and on record, but then had relocated to France, where her career as an international star really took off. It was a time when French culture was enjoying something of a vogue, initially because Hollywood, challenged by the onslaught of television, had lost its knack of producing global female stars, and had found itself outflanked by the appearance of Brigitte Bardot in *And God*

The Walker Brothers (opposite), an American band who were much bigger in Britain and who launched the career of the enigmatic Scott Walker (below).

Created Woman (1956). For a few years as the decade turned, it was French stars like Jeanne Moreau, Françoise Hardy and Catherine Deneuve who came to epitomize glamour, even as the books of the nouveau roman movement and the films of the nouvelle vague were exciting intellectuals and artists the world over. For some, France was an important counterweight to the American influence. 'America was still boss,' wrote British pop star Ian Whitcomb of his first trip to the USA in 1963, when he was still a student. 'For decades I'd dreamed of landing there and kissing the soil. Americans had better bodies, sculptured skulls. They *were* sex, I thought – next only to the French of course.'

There was, however, little corresponding interest in French music: Françoise Hardy became a familiar figure as a singer on British television, but Sacha Distel, Charles Aznavour and Gilbert Bécaud took another ten years and more before they made a chart impact over the Channel. The only real beneficiary was Petula Clark, who returned to London in 1964 to record 'Downtown' with producer Tony Hatch, a record that launched a new series of hits in Britain and gave her a #1 in America. Her subsequent releases owed as much to Broadway and to mainstream popular music as they did to contemporary styles; built around conventional orchestrations, they were less soulful than Dusty Springfield, less fashionable than Sandie Shaw, but just as powerful as either. Effortlessly finding a place for herself on television variety shows, she established that beat music hadn't destroyed the possibilities of pursuing a more orthodox showbiz career.

LEFT: Dionne Warwick, who started her long career as a backing singer on records by acts such as the Drifters.

RIGHT: Engelbert Humperdinck, the biggest British chart star of 1967.

BELOW LEFT: Esther and Abi Ofarim, a married couple from Israel whose 'Cinderella Rockefella' reached #1 in Britain in 1968.

Anita Harris, who came from the Cliff Adams Singers to have solo hits in 1967–68.

Following Clark came a string of others, working in a big ballad style that could appeal across age ranges, and benefitting from the result. Comedian Ken Dodd sold a million copies of his straight song 'Tears', and in 1967 – remembered for the summer of love, when the media were fixated upon psychedelia and flower power – the three biggest singles of the year were all by Engelbert Humperdinck: 'Release Me', 'There Goes My Everything' and 'Last Waltz'. Meanwhile established artists such as Shirley Bassey and Dionne Warwick may have found the charts temporarily less amenable but could always count on being welcomed in television studios. And Cilla Black emerged as easily the most durable Merseybeat star this side of the Beatles, progressing effortlessly from #1 hits in 1964 with 'Anyone Who Had a Heart' and 'You're My World' to headlining her own long-running TV series, *Cilla*, starting in 1968.

Somewhere between these unashamedly middle-of-the-road artists and the hipper end of the scene were the Walker Brothers, an American trio who arrived in London in 1965 and promptly struck a rich vein with 'Make It Easy on Yourself', 'My Ship Is Coming In' and 'The Sun Ain't Gonna Shine Anymore'. Drenched in massive orchestrations that borrowed from Phil Spector's work with the Righteous Brothers, they would by any normal standards have been seen as straightforward easy-listening, were it not for the fact that Scott Walker's baritone voice was so luscious, so atmospheric that there seemed to be hidden depths. When he turned out to be as moody in person as he was on record – citing Jacques Brel as his inspiration, when he wasn't shunning publicity altogether – the suspicion that he might be a serious artist, with aspirations beyond the charts, grew into a certainty, and he went on to pursue the most idiosyncratic career of any pop star.

The middle-of-the-road surge threatened at times to take over the charts but there were signs that the folk-rock tradition might still have a part to play, as when the London-born Cat Stevens became a star in 1967. Underneath the quirky arrangements of his records, seemingly intended to attract Donovan fans, was a precocious songwriting talent that was the closest Britain came to producing its own Paul Simon, though it was not until 1970 that he established his mature style. By then a new world was opening up for singer-songwriters. Drawing from country, blues and jazz, these new artists were essentially rooted in the personal and social lyrics bequeathed by Dylan, and like him they focused on both hit singles and album sales (Dylan had had three albums in the British charts before his first single achieved the same success). Mostly they were American but there was also room for an exceptional British talent like Labi Siffre to make his mark.

LEFT AND RIGHT:
Cat Stevens, who had
his first big hit in 1967 with
'Matthew and Son' and
became an international
star in the 1970s.

James Taylor, one of the
new generation of American
singer-songwriters to
emerge in the early 1970s.

RIGHT: Labi Siffre, whose hit songs included 'It Must Be Love' and 'Crying Laughing Loving Lying'.

LEFT: Don McLean, New York singer-songwriter whose 1972 'American Pie' summed up the story of rock and roll thus far.

BELOW RIGHT: Glen Campbell, a session musician and singer who became one of the few country acts to have mainstream hits in Britain.

Half-a-decade on from the folk-rock breakthrough, its legacy could still be discerned. That of the protest boom was much less visible. It was noticeable that when, in response to the 1968 Race Relations Act, the Conservative Party politician Enoch Powell made his apocalyptic 'rivers of blood' speech, advocating the repatriation of black and Asian immigrants to Britain, it was former mod heroine Millie Small who responded most vociferously with the song 'Enoch Power'. Meanwhile Manfred Mann Chapter Three, a group descended from the outfit who had recorded 'With God on Our Side' back in the dawn of protest, confined themselves to an instrumental track on their 1969 debut album titled 'Konekuf'. It was intended to be read backwards.

Neil Sedaka (right) and Neil Diamond (left), two of the most successful American singer-songwriters of the early 1970s.

OPPOSITE: Roberta Flack, who had solo hits as well as successful duets with Donny Hathaway.

chapter four

PURPLE HAZE

When Brian Epstein became manager of the Beatles, his motivation was not dissimilar to that of earlier rock and roll managers such as Larry Parnes or Joe Meek: as a gay businessman, he recognized attractive young men when he saw them and he reasonably calculated that others too would fall under their spell. The key difference was that where Parnes and Meek had concentrated on solo acts – Marty Wilde, Billy Fury, Heinz – Epstein found himself with a group, and the changed dynamic that resulted was one of the key factors in the subsequent evolution of pop. For where a single impressionable eighteen-year-old could be moulded and shaped by an older father figure, a group, and particularly one containing such wilful characters as John Lennon and Paul McCartney, proved much more resistant to managerial influence, having already established their own peer group relationship over several years of gigging.

So while the Beatles were prepared initially to go along with Epstein's attempts to conform to existing standards – abandoning their black leather in favour of matching suits, for example – their ability to dig their heels in became rapidly apparent, as in their early rejection of pantomime. By 1966, their attitudes strengthened by mixing with like-minded non-conformists, they were straying still further. 'We're more popular than Jesus now,' announced Lennon; 'I don't know which will go first – rock and roll or Christianity.' The response to his comment was, in some quarters, one of absolute outrage. 'The Beatles are not welcome in Memphis,' said the city commission, as public burnings of the band's records were staged in various southern states, and Epstein hurried to issue a humble apology: 'The Beatles will not, by word, action or otherwise, in any way offend or ridicule the religious beliefs of anyone throughout their forthcoming concert tour,' he insisted. 'John Lennon deeply and sincerely regrets any offence that he might have caused.' Lennon's own display of contrition was less convincing; on that final

OPPOSITE: P.P. Arnold.

American tour the band was asked about the Vietnam War, and he didn't seem concerned about causing further controversy: 'We think of it every day. We don't like it. We don't agree with it. We think it's wrong.' And again Epstein was distressed by the failure of his charges to follow showbiz etiquette.

The emergence of groups as the central relationship in pop was not always an easy path to navigate. Several musicians found themselves victims of internal coups as other band members took control, most notably the Rolling Stones, shaped early on by Brian Jones but falling under the leadership of Mick Jagger and Keith Richards as they began to write the material. Or else there was a phased takeover, as when the Alan Price Combo was renamed the Animals; Price subsequently left, the group soon dissolved and then re-emerged as a vehicle for its vocalist, Eric Burdon and the Animals. There was a fundamental instability that came with the claustrophobia of a group line-up, most famously evident in the splitting of the Beatles at the end of the decade but also seen in the fact that Eric Clapton got through four separate bands in the space of five years: the Yardbirds, John Mayall's Bluesbreakers, the Cream and Blind Faith.

Against these perhaps negative aspects, there was the strength that came with belonging to a gang, the power it gave the Beatles to chart their own course, despite their manager's more conservative instincts. Epstein was in some regards a transitional figure, wishing to cling to an older tradition, while being prepared to indulge and support the initiatives of his band. Those who followed were of a different breed: Andrew Loog Oldham was ten years younger than Epstein and, even more significant, he was younger than the Rolling Stones themselves, while others, particularly Chris Stamp and Kit Lambert with the Who and Tony Secunda with the Move, actively encouraged and promoted controversial behaviour. They weren't all as precocious as Oldham but they shared an attitude that combined art-school aesthetics with a barrow-boy sensibility. 'Secunda', wrote George Melly at the time, 'can stand as the most perfect specimen of all those ex-public-school layabouts who'd been sitting on their arses up and down the King's Road for almost a decade, wondering what to do with the only talent most of them had – an instinct for style.'

One of Secunda's scams was to prove extremely costly. The Move's 1967 single 'Flowers in the Rain' was promoted with a postcard sent to journalists that featured an allegedly pornographic drawing by Neil Smith, in the style of Aubrey Beardsley, that repeated a libellous rumour about Harold Wilson. Wilson promptly sued both the band and their manager (as well as the printers), retaining Conservative MP Quintin Hogg to represent him: 'The prime minister has, in fact, for some years

The Rolling Stones.

ABOVE LEFT: The Yardbirds.
Clockwise from top left:
Chris Dreja, Jim McCarty,
Keith Relf, Jeff Beck,
Jimmy Page.

ABOVE RIGHT: Jimmy Page.

OPPOSITE: Keith Relf.

been aware that various false and malicious rumours have been spread concerning his personal character and integrity.' It was the kind of litigious behaviour that didn't reflect particularly well on such a senior politician – Peter Cook once joked in his deadpan way that 'I suppose you could say that the biggest sue-er was Harold Wilson' – but the consequences were worse for the band: Wilson won the case and was awarded all the royalties from the record and the sheet music. He donated the money to charity, the Spastics Society and Stoke Mandeville Hospital.

By this stage, the energy that had driven the pop boom was dissipating, at least as far as the London elite were concerned. Although the quote about Jesus got the most attention, the more enduring impression given in that 1966 interview was Lennon's sheer weariness; isolated in his mansion in Weybridge, he appeared sunk in ennui, unable to find solace in material possessions and at a loss to know quite what to do with himself: 'We've never had time before to do anything but just be Beatles.' Ringo Starr was to echo the sentiments in another interview: 'I get bored like anyone else, but instead of having three hours a night, I have all day to get bored in,' he said, yearning for the certainties of the past. 'Sometimes I feel I'd like to stop being famous and get back to where I was in Liverpool.'

RIGHT AND BELOW:
The changing image
of Eric Clapton.

OPPOSITE: The Cream. From
left to right: Eric Clapton,
Ginger Baker, Jack Bruce.

OVERLEAF: Jimi Hendrix
backstage on two separate
visits to *Top of the Pops*.

Jimi Hendrix on stage at the New Century Hall, Manchester, 7 January 1967, a week after his debut on *Top of the Pops*.

The journalist who interviewed Lennon, Maureen Cleave, was to expand on the theme in London's *Evening Standard* at the end of 1966, drawing attention to the symbolism of the ending of *Ready Steady Go!* 'Nothing could disguise the fact that the pop scene that has diverted the general public for the last three years is over, finished and done with,' she wrote under the headline THE YEAR POP WENT FLAT. 'Paradoxically, the records are better than ever: the Who, the Kinks, the Hollies, the Beatles, the Stones and the Beach Boys have produced some splendid things; but the vigour, the freshness and the monstrous nerve have gone.' Writer Mick Farren agreed as he looked back on the time: 'All them hard bad-trip records came out,' he noted, citing the Stones' '19th Nervous Breakdown' and the Beatles' *Revolver*; 'everyone was sort of looking around wondering what the fuck was going on.'

The realization was dawning that the much-vaunted vanguard might not be representative of London, let alone of the rest of the country. Films like *Darling* (1965) and *I'll Never Forget What's 'is Name* (1967) were expressing cynicism about the entire concept of the swinging Sixties, while 'In Gear', a 1967 cinema short in the Rank Organization's *Look at Life* series, focused on London fashion and boutiques and opened with a flat statement of fact: 'They say London swings. It doesn't. Not even the King's Road, Chelsea. But here and there, among the conformist fat cat crowds is a lean cat or two, looking like it might swing, given some encouragement.'

Those who did choose to swing were increasingly favouring a new wave of boutiques, including I Was Lord Kitchener's Valet, which specialized in vintage uniforms from the military and the police, and Granny Takes a Trip, best known for its constantly changing and always spectacular

The Move. From left to right: Bev Bevan, Roy Wood, Carl Wayne, Rick Price.

OPPOSITE: Roy Wood, with Carl Wayne behind.

external decor. The longer established Hung On You was also keeping pace with the increasingly eclectic fashions, with a Mao jacket (called the Great Leap Forward) proving popular in the summer of 1967; indeed the fame of the shop had become such that it was reported that 'Scandinavian boutiques are already displaying signs announcing THE HUNG ON YOU STYLE.'

But still, as fashions became more extreme, as music got more experimental, as graphic design began to plunder the legacy of Beardsley and of the children's illustrator Mabel Lucie Attwell – many of these developments under the influence of increased drug use – the numbers in the front line of youth culture steadily reduced. 'The underground was terribly small, and very, very localized,' remembered disc jockey John Peel. Puzzled by the lack of success of the debut album by Country Joe and the Fish, 'I said to the record company, "Why isn't this in the charts? Everybody I know has a copy." But what I didn't realize was that it was the other way around: I knew everybody who'd got a copy.'

Some groups did break through. The Pink Floyd (the definite article was then part of their name), purveyed a sound that Peel famously described as being 'like cries of dying galaxies lost in sheer corridors of time and space' and led a break-out from London's underground circuit centred on the UFO Club and the Roundhouse; they even scored a couple of hit singles, before adopting an albums-only policy. The Beatles (triumphantly) and the Stones (unconvincingly) adapted their sound and image, moving further away from simple rock and roll, while the Yardbirds, who should have been in the forefront after revolutionary 1966 hits with 'Shapes of Things' and 'Over Under Sideways Down', got lost as a result of poor record company support. Meanwhile their former guitarist, Eric Clapton, had formed the first of the so-called supergroups in the shape of the Cream, whose extended on-stage soloing didn't preclude them from releasing hit singles. Most striking of all was the arrival from America of Jimi Hendrix, whose extraordinary guitar playing was first experienced on television in the penultimate edition of *Ready Steady Go!* and made an immediate impact.

Amongst those affected by this wave of what had become known as psychedelia was the formerly raucous Eric Burdon, now relocated to San Francisco and reborn as a flower power penitent. 'When I was drinking, I should have been thinking,' he sang on his hit 'Good Times' in 1967; 'All of that boozing, I was really losing.' As he later explained: 'LSD came along and the music suddenly went all trippy and dreamy and flowers that grow so incredibly high. Everything became much softer, much more hallucinogenic, trippy, dreamy.' Another R&B singer, Stevie Winwood, formerly of the Spencer Davis Group, re-emerged in Traffic, singing about elephant's eyes and bubblegum trees.

Not everyone was impressed. With neither the profile nor the inclination to participate, Peter Noone found his band being sneered at by some of the new San Franciscan acts: 'They were down on Herman's Hermits because we were a pop act and we didn't know where Vietnam was,' he recalled. Pete Quaife, bassist with the Kinks, one of the few groups who successfully ignored the entire psychedelic fad, was more forthright: 'It changed a lot of good blokes, who everybody rated, into creeps.'

And the truth was that despite all the column inches lavished on the new music, it never really translated into corresponding sales. Two of the definitive pieces of British psychedelia in 1967 – Tomorrow's 'My White Bicycle' and the Pretty Things' 'Defecting Grey' – simply failed to chart, without any album success to compensate their makers. Even the Beatles' *Sgt Pepper's Lonely Hearts Club Band*, instantly recognized as a classic almost everywhere (except

Otis Redding, whose cover of the Stones' 'Satisfaction' and whose appearance at the 1967 Monterey Pop Festival made him the biggest soul star amongst rock audiences.

in the journal of the Young Communist League, where it was mocked as *Sgt Pep-Up's Phoney Thoughts Club Band*), was outsold that year by the soundtrack album to *The Sound of Music*.

If the real thing didn't find it easy to win over audiences, there was also some muddying of the waters with a spate of fakedelic records, defined as music 'designed to take the mickey out of, or cash in on, psychedelia'. Some of these records were deliberate exploitation fare, as with songwriters John Carter and Ken Lewis, formerly of beat group the Ivy League, who created 'Let's Go to San Francisco' under the name the Flower Pot Men, and then invented a band to promote it. Another song writing team, Ken Howard and Alan Blaikley, also kept pace with records by Dave Dee, Dozy, Beaky, Mick and Tich and by the Herd – the latter scoring with 'From the Underworld' and 'Paradise Lost', which drew on the myth of Orpheus and the work of John Milton respectively. Others just fitted the mood, whether intentionally or not: the Troggs, the most gloriously primitive of all British beat bands, released 'Night of the Long Grass' (a bucolic romance that wasn't about drugs) and 'Love Is All Around' (a song of sexual frustration), and found they slotted into 1967 quite nicely. Similarly the Status Quo made their debut with 'Pictures of Matchstick Men' and were promptly taken shopping in Carnaby Street by their management so they could look suitably up-to-the-minute on *Top of the Pops*.

Brian Jones of the Rolling Stones at the peak of his psychedelic dandy image.

In a slightly different category were the Move, who had made a name for themselves with a stage act that echoed the Who's smashing up of their instruments – they went in for attacking TV sets – but who benefited from the magpie genius of songwriter Roy Wood; he could turn his hand to almost any style of music and did so effortlessly with psychedelia. And then there were the Bee Gees, newly arrived from Australia, whose first album, released in 1967, contained not only solid gold pop songs in 'To Love Somebody' and 'New York Mining Disaster 1941', but also more immediately fashionable fare: 'Cucumber Castle', 'Red Chair, Fade Away', 'Every Christian Lion Hearted Man Will Show You'.

The Bee Gees backstage with their parents and their younger brother, Andy Gibb.

RIGHT: The Bee Gees.
From left to right:
Barry Gibb, Colin Petersen,
Robin Gibb, Vince Melouney,
Maurice Gibb.

OPPOSITE: The Bee Gees on *Top of the Pops* – it was on the show that Maurice Gibb met his future wife Lulu.

None of these was any more genuinely psychedelic than were Drimble Wedge and the Vegetations in Peter Cook and Dudley Moore's 1967 film *Bedazzled*, nor did they depend on the ingestion of LSD for inspiration. 'I didn't even know how to spell "psychedelic" back then,' remarked Francis Rossi of the Status Quo, and Chris Britton, guitarist with the Troggs, agreed: 'None of us were drug mad; we had enough trouble with beer and Scotch.' Even so, all contributed to a brief period when backwards tapes, faux-naïve lyrics and sitar flourishes seemed eminently sensible additions to pop music. But it was brief,

Barry (left), Robin (centre) and Maurice Gibb (right).

its peak spanning just the summer months of 1967, when the charts were dominated by three consecutive #1 hits that encapsulated the period: Procul Harum's 'A Whiter Shade of Pale', the Beatles' 'All You Need Is Love' and Scott McKenzie's 'San Francisco (Be Sure to Wear Some Flowers in Your Hair)'. This trio, however, was immediately followed by Engelbert Humperdinck's 'The Last Waltz', as though in farewell to the summer of flower power.

Running alongside this expansion of what pop could and should do came a clash between youth culture and the forces of the establishment. The chief constable of Manchester had already waged a war against the clubs where the music had originated (an internal police report described the habitués of these clubs as 'individuals of exaggerated dress and deportment, commonly known as mods, rockers or beatniks'), and had successfully lobbied for the Manchester

Corporation Act of 1965, which gave his force new powers to regulate the establishments. That legislation was then used as the basis of the 1968 Private Places of Entertainment (Licensing) Act, which was introduced to parliament by the Lord Chief Justice, Hubert Parker, in a headmasterly tone: 'These clubs naturally attract the young and those of a more disreputable nature, in particular those with no fixed abode, abscondees from approved schools and other institutions, as well as those who desire to escape supervision by their parents, and indeed supervision by any adult control.' He added that the clubs were notorious for the use of drugs: 'True, most of these were of the Indian hemp, "purple heart" and other drugs of the amphetamine class, but activities were certainly not confined to those and extended to heroin, cocaine and morphia.'

Even in this context, though, some clubs were too sacred to hit. The Cavern in Liverpool, where the Beatles had built their reputation, was closed in early 1966 by bailiffs, but was reopened later in the year by none other than Harold Wilson. 'There is a tendency to decry youth,' he intoned, as he did the honours, 'or to sensationalize the actions of a small and scruffy minority who carry liberty beyond licence to dangerous and self-destructive addictions and other forms of getting kicks in the seamier purlieus of London's nightlife, a problem which, I may say, the home secretary is making a drive to clean up. But these people, and other delinquents, are not typical in any way of Britain's youth.'

The attacks on youth culture were scarcely new, for those in authority had long worried about places where young people congregated. The coffee bars of the previous decade had also attracted official disapproval and, going further back, one commentator, writing in the 1890s, had thundered that he would 'rather see a young man hanging about a public house than spending his time in these places.' The places that were then so distressing to decent-minded folk were the newly created public libraries, where the working classes, it was feared, would spend their time 'perusing light literature' instead of seeking gainful employment.

But there were novel aspects in the mid 1960s, particularly in the focus on drugs, whether hard or soft. Convictions for the possession of cannabis rose fourfold in the years 1965–67, reflecting a greater enthusiasm on the part of both those who wished to use it and those who wished to see it suppressed. The most famous drug convictions were those of Brian Jones, Mick Jagger and Keith Richards in 1967; they received custodial sentences ranging from three months to a year, though all were set aside on appeal. The high profile of the cases provoked Richard Hamilton into breaking with his normal American subjects to produce a screen print, *Swingeing London '67*, based on a photograph of

Dave Dee, Dozy, Beaky, Mick and Tich. Clockwise from top left: Ian 'Tich' Amey, Dave Dee, Anthony 'Beaky' Carpenter, Trevor 'Dozy' Ward-Davies, John 'Mick' Hatchman.

OPPOSITE: Radio One DJ Alan Freeman with Gary Taylor and (right) Peter Frampton of the Herd.

BELOW: Reg Presley (left) and Peter Frampton (right), lead singers with the Troggs and the Herd respectively.

Mick Jagger and art dealer Robert Frazer in the back of a police car. It also produced a supportive editorial, WHO BREAKS A BUTTERFLY ON A WHEEL?, written by William Rees-Mogg, the comparatively youthful (he was thirty-three) editor of *The Times*. The underground equivalent to that newspaper, the *International Times*, sought comfort in the face of the state's onslaught: 'No matter how many raids and arrests the police make on whatever pretence, there can be no final bust because the revolution has taken place *within the minds* of the young.'

That was perhaps a little optimistic, but certainly seeds had been sown that would grow and would one day flower, even if in some cases it would not be until the 1980s that they did so and even if that flowering was to take some strange and unpredictable forms. In the meantime, there was rejoicing in the record industry that sales of albums were soaring – helped by the fact that prices had remained static for four years – and that where in 1963–65 there had been effectively just one marketplace, there were now many, increasing the chances of making profits. After the strange summer of 1967, wrote manager Simon Napier-Bell, 'the music business had changed for good. A new tough professionalism had taken over, and the money to be made was greater than ever.'

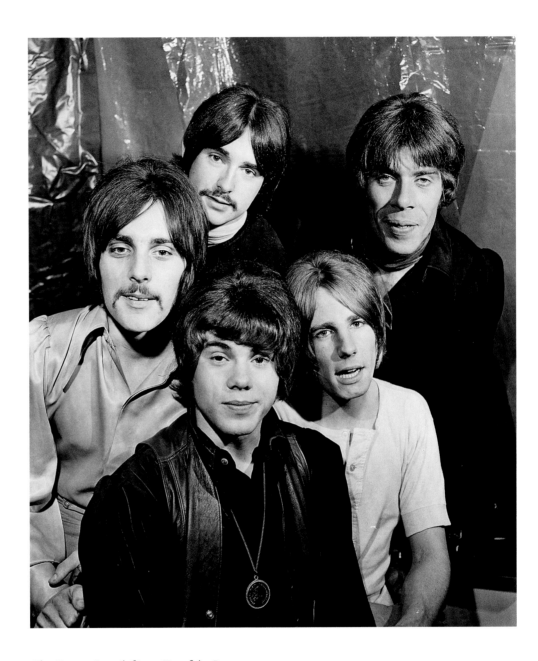

The Status Quo (left) on *Top of the Pops*
with Harry Goodwin
(photograph by Ron Howard) and (above)
backstage. Clockwise from left: John
Coghlan, Francis 'Mike' Rossi, Roy Lynes,
Rick Parfitt, Alan Lancaster.

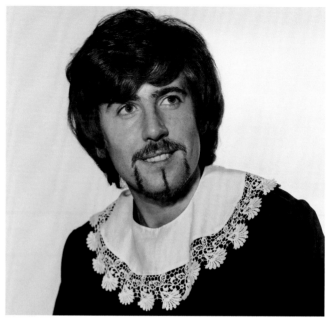

The changing face of Graham Nash of the Hollies.

OPPOSITE: The Radha Krishna Temple whose 'Hare Krishna Mantra' was a hit single on the Beatles' Apple label.

At the end of 1967 Bob Harris, future presenter of *The Old Grey Whistle Test*, wrote in an edition of *Unit*, the student magazine of Keele University: 'Pop music seems to be splitting in two. In one direction Engelbert and his mimics rush away with their adoring fans, whilst towards the other extreme, various groups and individuals led by the Beatles progress to a freer, improvised and distinctively creative sphere.' In fact, the split was greater than that. The easy-listening boom symbolized by Humperdinck was to continue, but rock and roll itself had split with, on the one hand, singles-based acts aiming for a younger, predominantly female audience and, on the other, albums-based bands looking to the older, more male end of the market. The latter were, inevitably, to get most of the critical attention and to prove the more fashionable. The book *Bluff Your Way in Social Climbing*, published in spring 1967, offered tips for the right names to drop in the best social circles – the Beatles, Mick Jagger, the Small Faces and the Walker Brothers – but it added that those for the future included the Cream, Donovan, the Move and the Pink Floyd. It also suggested that Brian Epstein was the pop manager for today, with Tony Secunda for tomorrow.

Epstein didn't live long enough to be so eclipsed. He died of a drugs overdose in August 1967, one of three key figures in British pop culture to die shockingly young that year, following the suicide of record producer Joe Meek and the murder of playwright Joe Orton. All were gay and all died within a few weeks of the passing of the Sexual Offences Act that legalized, within certain limits, male homosexuality.

chapter five

WON'T GET FOOLED AGAIN

I n the struggle by the establishment to curb what it saw as the wilder excesses of youth culture, perhaps the most contentious issue of all was that of broadcasting and of the pirate radio stations. Prior to 1964, British radio had offered a simple choice for pop fans: there was the BBC's Light Programme, which devoted as little time as it could get away with to rock and roll, beyond the two hours allocated to Brian Matthew and *Saturday Club*, and there was Radio Luxembourg, much of the airtime on which was paid for by the big four record companies – Decca, EMI, Philips and Pye – to promote their music. There were no local stations, which is one of the reasons why the northern beat boom had come as such a shock to the record industry, and no independent stations.

Of the two available options, Luxembourg was the popular choice, and had been as far back as the 1930s, when it had the reputation, in Ian Whitcomb's words, for 'culture-free programmes such as *Littlewood's Pools Broadcast* with records by Gracie Fields, George Formby, Billy Cotton'. But its signal couldn't always be relied upon, and anyway it was as staid in its non-music policy as the BBC, specifically banning: 'References, jokes or songs concerning any reigning monarch, members of parliament, the cabinet or any branch of Her Majesty's government or any other government, politics or political figures, subjects that may be regarded as having an indirect political significance nationally or internationally, religion, other advertisers, physical deformities, or any other reference, joke or song considered to be in questionable taste.' There was no room here for anyone whose sympathies lay with the satire boom.

And then came an Irish entrepreneur, Ronan O'Rahilly, founder of the Scene Club in London, who conceived the idea of broadcasting from a ship just outside British territorial waters and therefore beyond the scope of the government. On

OPPOSITE: Alvin Lee of blues-rock band Ten Years After.

ABOVE LEFT: Christine Perfect of British blues band Chicken Shack and later of Fleetwood Mac.

ABOVE RIGHT: Bob 'the Bear' Hite, singer with American blues band Canned Heat.

OPPOSITE : Billy Preston, one of the most in-demand session musicians, who played on the Beatles' 'Get Back' as well as having solo hits.

Easter Sunday 1964 – the date, said O'Rahilly, was chosen because his grandfather had died fighting the British in the Easter Rising of 1916 – Radio Caroline took to the air and began to broadcast non-stop pop. Other so-called pirate stations swiftly followed the lead, most famously Radio London but also Radios City, King, Victor, England, Scotland and Britain amongst others, some broadcasting from ships, others from abandoned fortifications out in the Thames Estuary. They were an instant success, claiming a listenership of 20 million, and they were funded partly by record companies paying for airplay and partly by advertising, often from unexpectedly establishment clients – the first advert on Caroline was for Woburn Abbey, the family seat of the Duke of Bedford, followed by the likes of the National Coal Board, the Egg Marketing Board, Royal Ascot and even the police; the station claimed that in its first eighteen months it grossed £750,000 through advertising.

All of this was perfectly legal but was frowned upon by the formidable forces ranged against the pirates. They included the BBC, who didn't like losing their monopoly or being made to look out of touch; the newspapers and commercial television channels, who felt their advertising base was being threatened; the Musicians' Union, who objected to there being no live work for their members; and the record industry, offended by the promotion of new independent record labels and 'convinced that if hit records were played too many times, people

wouldn't bother to go out and buy them' (the fall in the number of singles sold as the pirates got big offered some evidence for this). Most significant of all was the left wing of the Labour Party, which believed that broadcasting was too important to be let out of state control; it had objected to the introduction of commercial television in the 1950s and would do so again in the 1970s with commercial radio – it was hardly likely to take to the idea of the pirates, who didn't even pay tax.

Leading this group was Anthony Wedgwood Benn, a former BBC employee who was now postmaster general in the Labour government, with responsibility for broadcasting policy. (The fact that Radios England and Britain were based on a ship named *Laissez Faire* seemed almost designed to infuriate Benn, one of the keenest advocates of a fully planned economy.) When he took office in October

OPPOSITE: Peter Green, who replaced Eric Clapton in John Mayall's Bluesbreakers and later formed Fleetwood Mac (below).

Fleetwood Mac, at the time of their #1 hit 'Albatross'. From left to right: Mick Fleetwood, Peter Green, John McVie, Danny Kirwan, Jeremy Spencer.

OPPOSITE: Ian Anderson, singer and flautist with Jethro Tull.

1964, he was told by his civil servants that 'legislation was at an advanced stage of development on the radio pirates' with the aim of 'making it illegal to advertise or to supply pirates with certain services'. By May 1966 there had been no progress and he was becoming impatient: 'I have tried to get a pirate Bill into the legislative programme in three separate sessions,' he fretted, 'and the cabinet had got cold feet, with Harold Wilson having the coldest of all. He enjoys the pirates and has always been trying to find some way of taxing them. This of course would be guaranteed to consolidate their strength and the Treasury would then never let us kill them.' The prime minister, it appeared, was a particular fan of Radio 390, an easy-listening station.

The situation was to be transformed by an incident the very next month. In June 1966 Major Oliver Smedley, who had formerly owned Radio Atlanta, forcibly repossessed from Reg Calvert, the head of Radio City, a transmitter that had apparently not been paid for. The next day Calvert visited Smedley at the latter's home in Saffron Walden and in an altercation was shot dead by the retired army officer. 'Gangsterism has moved into the pirates and the government's failure to act is now an absolute disgrace,' fumed Benn in his diary. Smedley was initially charged with murder, which was then reduced to manslaughter, and at his trial in October was acquitted on the grounds of self-defence. The jury didn't feel the need to retire to consider their verdict, and Smedley was awarded

Marsha Hunt, actress and singer, whose first hit came with a cover of Dr John's 'I Walk on Gilded Splinters'.

some of his defence costs. But by that stage, the damage had already been done: amidst a media backlash against the pirates, the Marine &c. Broadcasting (Offences) Bill had been published and was well on its way to becoming law.

'One has to be wary of conspiracy theories,' noted Johnnie Walker, former disc jockey on Caroline, 'but the facts are these: that Reg Calvert was shot, Oliver Smedley pulled the trigger, Oliver Smedley got off.' He added: 'It was only after that murder and court case that the Labour government felt able to push through a law that would turn off the pirates, so one has to be extremely suspicious of that whole murder and court case and everything that followed on.'

Thunderclap Newman, whose single 'Something in the Air' was #1 at the time of the first Moon landing. From left to right: Andy 'Thunderclap' Newman and Jimmy McCulloch, with Radio One DJ Dave Eager.

The Act that was passed sought to cut off the supply lines of the pirates by making it illegal to work for, to promote or to supply an offshore radio station; most significantly of all, it made advertising on offshore stations illegal, leaving the pirates without a revenue stream. The law came into effect at midnight on 14 August 1967 and virtually all the major stations accordingly ceased operations, with Radio London going off air that afternoon, and with Radio Scotland ending to the sound of a bagpipe lament. The one major exception was Radio Caroline, which announced that it would defy the new legislation and continue broadcasting, a decision that attracted massive media interest; at midnight Johnnie Walker played 'We Shall Overcome' to an audience of around 22 million in Britain and northern Europe. Thereafter it was harassed at every turn and the listener figures went into steep decline.

The pirates had had many faults, some technical, others born of timidity – Radio London had banned the Pink Floyd's debut single, 'Arnold Layne', because it was about clothes fetishism, and most of them banned Kim Fowley's fakedelic classic 'The Trip'. ('Taking a trip', explained *The Times*, when reporting this development, 'is a slang phrase for being under the influence of drugs.') But, even if one doesn't entirely accept O'Rahilly's argument that the pirates were 'part of a revolution against the entire forces of the establishment', they undoubtedly made a profound difference to broadcasting in Britain. Six weeks after the pirates were mostly driven off air, the BBC expanded and rebranded its radio services, adding a new station, Radio One, which was intended as a replacement for those that had been lost. It used jingles for the first time on the BBC, as pioneered by the pirates, it recruited many of its disc jockeys from the former stations and played nothing but pop music, opening with the Move's 'Flowers in the Rain' (from which, of course, the band didn't benefit). It was virtually the only show in town and it rapidly entrenched itself as the self-proclaimed 'nation's favourite', transforming the old image of Auntie Beeb into, in the words of the *Sunday Mirror*, that of 'a flower-powered swinging chick in a micro-skirt'.

There was, however, some dissatisfaction amongst the album-oriented end of rock, a feeling that the BBC, despite the creation of Radio One, was still not keeping up with developments in the music. For there was now emerging a new culture with groups expecting to be considered as serious artists, freed from the fripperies of pure pop: 'I don't want to be a clown any more,' Jimi Hendrix announced in 1969; 'I don't want to be a "rock and roll star."' He and others who sought to transcend teen-pop found a ready audience that was largely drawn from the ever-increasing

Colin Blunstone (left) and Curtis Mayfield (right), former singers with the Zombies and the Impressions respectively, who went on to successful solo careers.

OPPOSITE: Mike McGear
and Vivian Stanshall,
former members of the
Scaffold and the Bonzo
Dog Band respectively.

ranks of students and graduates, the beneficiaries of the expansion of tertiary
education in Britain, which had seen student numbers double during the 1960s.

By the time Hendrix made his protest at not being taken seriously, the
parameters had been effectively laid down. The baroque excesses of 1967 had
provoked a reaction from within the music, a search to reconnect with what was
considered a more authentic, gritty tradition, even if there was no agreement on
quite what this meant. There was a revival of interest in electric blues, building on
the successes of Eric Clapton's work with John Mayall and in the Cream – in 1968
debut albums by Fleetwood Mac and Chicken Shack made the charts – but there
was also a return to folk music for inspiration: Bob Dylan's album *John Wesley
Harding* turned its back on his recent electric sounds, while in Britain Fairport
Convention came out of the underground clubs to launch a new era of folk-rock.
There was also in 1968 a step back to an earlier rock and roll attitude, particularly
on the part of Britain's two leading bands: the Rolling Stones entered their most
celebrated period with the single 'Jumpin' Jack Flash', while the Beatles' 'Lady
Madonna' borrowed both from Fats Domino and from Humphrey Lyttelton's 'Bad
Penny Blues', the first home-grown hit of the trad jazz era, twelve years earlier.

The most successful
incarnation of the
Moody Blues. From left
to right: Justin Hayward,
Ray Thomas, Graeme Edge
(seated), Mike Pinder,
John Lodge.

What was characteristic of all these trends was their myopic focus on the music. The political protests and upheavals of 1968 in the communist countries, in America and in France had their echoes in Britain – primarily in the clashes with the police outside the American Embassy in London – but they had little resonance inside rock. Instead there was a withdrawal from politics: on *The Beatles*, John Lennon rejected in 'Revolution 1' the then fashionable iconography of Mao Zedong, while George Harrison's 'While My Guitar Gently Weeps'

OPPOSITE: Free. From left to right: Simon Kirke, Paul Kossoff (standing), Andy Fraser, Paul Rodgers.

The final version of the Move. From left to right: Roy Wood, Bev Bevan, Jeff Lynne.

RIGHT: The Electric Light
Orchestra, formed by
Roy Wood, Jeff Lynne and
Bev Bevan as a successor
to the Move, though Wood
left after the first album.

Blue Mink, featuring singer
Madeline Bell (centre) and
bassist Herbie Flowers
(far left), who had a long
string of hits starting with
'Melting Pot' in 1969.

ABOVE AND OPPOSITE: Solo Beatles, George Harrison (above) and John Lennon (opposite).

FOLLOWING PAGES: The Rolling Stones in the early 1970s, with Mick Taylor, second left, (pages 158-9) having replaced Brian Jones, and the Who (pages 162-3) in the same period.

sounded a retreat into introspection. The Stones too made their choice of music over revolution explicit with 'Street Fighting Man', and the tendency culminated in the Who's 1971 classic 'Won't Get Fooled Again'. ('It's a terrible song,' Pete Townshend said, years later; 'it's saying: There's no point in having anything to do with politics and revolution, because it's all a lot of nonsense.')

The turn away from political involvement was perhaps inevitable as a decade of clamour and change drew to a close, and the realization dawned that, despite all the rhetoric, the power structures against which so many had railed remained absolutely intact. Indeed there was a wave of reaction around much of the world, a swing to the right that was heralded by the election of Ronald Reagan as governor of California at the start of 1967. The following year, Richard M. Nixon was elected American president and Charles de Gaulle won the French parliamentary elections by a landslide. To complete the pattern, in 1970 Harold Wilson was unexpectedly swept out of office by a Conservative Party led by Edward Heath, a grammar-school modernizer very much in Wilson's image (he was 'the first Tory leader with wall-to-wall carpeting' gushed *The Sunday Times*). Not all in the pop industry were upset by this latter development. 'It is a little known fact', claimed the disc jockey Emperor Rosko, 'that the Ted Heath government would never have come to power if it hadn't been for Radio Caroline, who devoted a certain period for three months prior to the election to "Vote in the Conservatives", because they were going to legalise pirate radio. He started gaining from the day that started being broadcast.'

But while the songs eschewed engagement, the music was increasingly seen by commentators as the soundtrack of the times, nowhere more so than in the 1968 BBC documentary *All My Loving*. When film-maker Tony Palmer proposed a programme about the kind of rock bands celebrated by critics, he found encouragement from John Lennon 'because there is an increasing number of musicians who simply cannot get onto the BBC.' From the vantage point of 30 years on, Palmer explained that '*Top of the Pops* consisted of, as it were, Tommy Steele and Cliff Richard,' and that he wanted to reflect the more thoughtful side of the industry. He did so with the aid of visuals showing concentration camp victims, police violence and a civilian being shot dead in Vietnam, a not wholly successful marriage of subject and soundtrack, despite Palmer's claims to objectivity: 'It is not for me to inflict an interpretation on you,' he declared. Mary Whitehouse complained, inevitably, but mostly it was well received; George Melly wrote in the *Observer* that: 'It said more about pop than a year of *Top of the Pops*, that dated weekly essay in nobility and careless superlatives.'

OPPOSITE: Curved Air. From left to right: Ian Eyre, Darryl Way, Sonja Kristina, Florian Pilkington-Miksa, Francis Monkman.

Black Sabbath. From left to right: Ozzy Osbourne, Geezer Butler, Bill Ward, Tony Iommi.

The fact that Palmer's film was repeatedly referred to in the context of *Top of the Pops* was an indication of the programme's continued dominance of televised pop. Yet even that show was exhibiting a certain nervousness, in the face of a continued decline in singles sales (in 1968 they dipped below the level they had been at when rock and roll first arrived) and the growing strength of the albums market. In response the show briefly adopted in 1971 an album slot, to allow, for example, a ten-minute song by the progressive-rock band Yes to be performed in its entirety. The experiment wasn't a conspicuous success – this wasn't the kind of entertainment that families expected or appreciated at 7.30 pm – and was swiftly abandoned, a process made easier by the arrival later that year of *The Old Grey Whistle Test* over on BBC2; as its most famous presenter, Bob Harris, summarized the situation: 'Top of the Pops was the singles show, we were the album show.' Even *Top of the Pops*, though, had its detractors amongst the more conservative elements within the BBC; in 1970 the comedy writer David Croft was invited to apply for the job of head of BBC television light

ABOVE LEFT: Deep Purple. From left to right: Ritchie Blackmore, Roger Glover, Ian Paice, Ian Gillan, Jon Lord.

ABOVE RIGHT: Emerson, Lake and Palmer. From left to right: Carl Palmer, Greg Lake, Keith Emerson.

OPPOSITE : Geordie, whose singer Brian Johnson (far left) went on to join AC/DC.

entertainment, but turned down the offer, partly because he didn't approve of much of the corporation's output: 'I thought *Top of the Pops* was encouraging the yob culture, but nobody would thank me for changing it.'

The new division of popular music into rock albums and pop singles forced existing bands to decide on which side of the fence they should fall. The Small Faces had evolved rapidly from a mod R&B band and were now making convincing albums, but they were also scoring hits with unrepresentative singles ('Itchycoo Park', 'Lazy Sunday') and starting to worry about what would happen when their pop appeal faded: 'The Small Faces' whole scene on stage was being screamed at,' remembered singer Steve Marriott. 'The louder the screams, the bigger you knew you were. When the screaming began to die down a bit, we began to feel very insecure.' But he didn't stay around long enough to find out what happened next; frustrated by their inability to address the subtleties of their #1 album, *Ogden's Nut Gone Flake*, in concert whilst the screaming continued, Marriott left the group at the start of 1969 and formed Humble Pie, a more straightforward hard rock band, with Peter Frampton, another escaping teen star who had formerly been with the Herd. (The tension between rock attitude and pop-star status was evident in the fact that, despite the hits, the Small Faces allegedly received an unofficial ban from *Top of the Pops* after an incident in which Marriott told producer Johnnie Stewart to 'fuck off'.)

King Crimson. From left to right:
Peter Giles, Keith Tippett,
Greg Lake, Michael Giles and
(seated) Robert Fripp on their
only *Top of the Pops* appearance.

RIGHT: The Strawbs. From left
to right: Blue Weaver, John Ford,
Dave Cousins, Dave Lambert
and (seated) Richard Hudson.

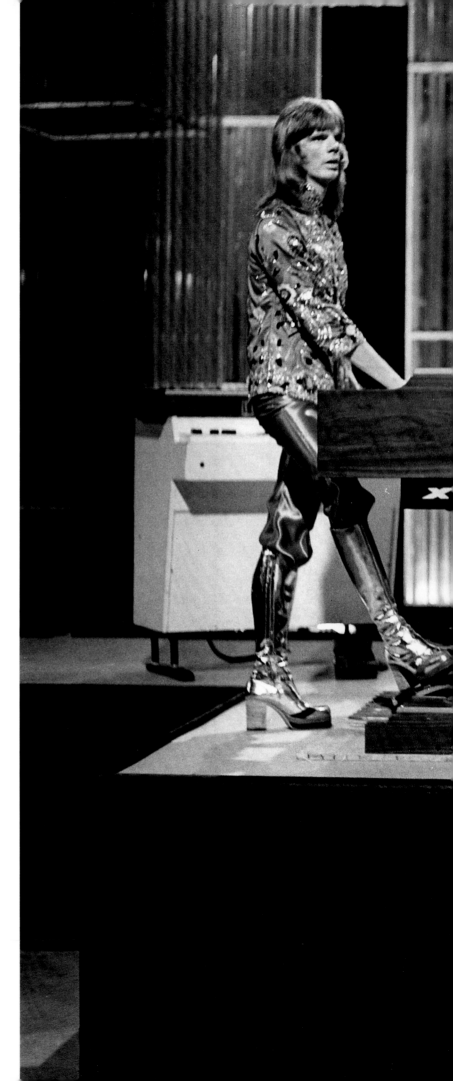

Humble Pie found more success in America than they did at home, an increasingly common experience following the second British invasion that had started in 1967, with the Cream, the Who and Jimi Hendrix blazing a trail for a heavier, less family-friendly brand of rock. Biggest of all proved to be Led Zeppelin, the band formed by guitarist Jimmy Page when he found that he was the last Yardbird standing. Their first two albums were released in 1969 and, supported by extensive touring of the States, they ended the year with the second of them at #1 in the American charts and with the accompanying single, 'Whole Lotta Love', making its way up to the top five. Although an instrumental version of that song, by Alexis Korner's band CCS, was to become the best known theme tune to *Top of the Pops*, Zeppelin never appeared on the show, steadfastly refusing to release any singles at all in Britain. In January 1970 Pink Floyd – who, in keeping with the prevailing fashion, had dropped the definite article from their name – announced that they would pursue the same policy, as did Black Sabbath later that year, after having a hit with 'Paranoid'.

Others were less precious, so that, for example, the American blues band Canned Heat could have a hit single on both sides of the Atlantic with 'Going Up the Country', even though it was taken from a double album containing one track, 'Refried Boogie', that lasted for over 40 minutes. And Free, possibly the best of the blues-based British bands, could quite happily pursue album and single sales simultaneously. But elsewhere the division had taken hold. Within heavy metal, and more particularly its chief rival, progressive rock, track lengths expanded, time signatures departed from the traditional 4/4 with a propensity to change frequently within a song, and artists began to aspire to the status of classical musicians. Not only singles were left behind; so too, in many cases, were albums as previously understood – double albums became common and even, in the cases of Yes and Emerson, Lake and Palmer, triple albums.

It wasn't simply a snobbish disregard for younger fans that had produced this attitude of scorning the traditional route to success via the singles charts. The screaming that did for the Small Faces was not unique to them, as the Kinks' *Live at Kelvin Hall* demonstrates – recorded in 1967, it is hard at times to hear the band through the noise of the audience adulation. The Beatles responded simply by abandoning live performance altogether, their last British gig being at the *New Musical Express* Pollwinners' Concert at Wembley in 1966, and their last ever at Candlestick Park, San Francisco later that year. The Rolling Stones likewise gave up on concerts for a while. Both groups, in the words of Pink Floyd manager Peter Jenner, 'had come to the position where they couldn't play live

Uriah Heep. Clockwise from top left: David Byron, Mick Box, Gary Thain, Ken Hensley, Lee Kerslake.

OPPOSITE: Thin Lizzy. From left to right: Gary Moore, Brian Downey, Phil Lynott.

The most successful line-up of Thin Lizzy. From left to right: Brian Downey, Brian Robertson, Phil Lynott, Scott Gorham.

any more. The PAs weren't loud enough to drown the screaming girls. So they had this problem of re-entry. The Beatles never solved it, but the Stones, and Jagger in particular, sussed it out.'

The 're-entry' for the Stones came at their free concert in London's Hyde Park in July 1969, just two days after the death of their founder, Brian Jones. He had already left the group, to be replaced by Mick Taylor, and his death prefaced a traumatic fifteen months for rock and roll. A subsequent free gig by the Stones at the Altamont speedway track in California ended in chaos as Hell's Angels, recruited to provide security, stabbed an audience member to death. ('Looking back, I don't think it was a good idea to have Hell's Angels there,' mused Keith Richards.) The band again went into temporary withdrawal. They released no new material at all in 1970, the year that the Beatles finally announced that they'd split up, and the year that the deaths were announced of Jimi Hendrix and Janis Joplin. When John Lennon sang 'the dream is over' in his 1970 song 'God', it seemed as though he was simply articulating an undeniable truth.

Dressing
Rooms
24 to 29

Dressing Room

chapter six

THOSE WERE THE DAYS

The physical format in which rock and roll was delivered had been in a state of flux from the outset. Originally the ten-inch 78 rpm disc was the favoured form, but by 1958 the seven-inch 45 rpm single had achieved sales parity, and from then on the 78 was clearly doomed. The seven-inch, four-track EP (extended play) was popular for a while in the early 1960s, but that too went into decline, and the last EP chart was published in *Record Retailer* in December 1967. The following year sales of twelve-inch 33 rpm long player albums reached the same level as singles and then overtook them.

The chart statistics for 1970 tell the story of the decline in importance of the single in Britain. It could be seen in terms of sales: of the 100 bestselling singles of the 1970s, just six came out in 1970, only three of which were British, and two of those weren't exactly cutting-edge pop – Clive Dunn's 'Grandad' and a bagpipe-led instrumental version of 'Amazing Grace' by the Band of the Royal Scots Dragoon Guards. It could also be seen in terms of the separation between rock and pop: half of the twenty bestselling albums of 1970 were by British acts, but the eight acts responsible could between them only muster five singles that even made the top 50 that year – the Beatles' 'Let It Be', Deep Purple's 'Black Night', the Moody Blues' 'Question', Black Sabbath's 'Paranoid' and Free's 'All Right Now'.

Also in 1970, for the first time since the show's inception, *Top of the Pops* failed to make the weekly charts of the top twenty most watched programmes at any stage during a calendar year, and it began to seem almost as though singles-based pop might wither on the vine from lack of interest. Worse still, the problem was institutionalized and self-perpetuating. With record companies chasing album sales, they had become indulgent of rock bands who would spend six months in the studio jamming, writing and recording a new LP, and they began to see the singles market simply as a way to make a quick profit and thus subsidize this leisurely lifestyle.

OPPOSITE: The Four Tops.

Consequently there arose what was effectively a return to the values of
Tin Pan Alley. Songwriting and production teams – Roger Cook and Roger
Greenaway, Barry Mason and Tony Macaulay, Bill Martin and Phil Coulter –
would produce hit singles on so tight a budget that they became a production
line. On those records, a small roster of session musicians filled the vacuum left
by the disappearance from the singles charts of the big-name bands. 'The
finances of making a record meant that for a pop single you needed to make it in
three hours,' remembered Ron Roker, one of the songwriters of the time. 'You'd
have three songs in that session: one was the A-side, one was the B-side, the
other was a possible A-side. And a lot of our music was made in those sessions
with the same guys because you knew what you were going to get: you could put
any dots in front of them.'

Session players had been part of rock and roll from the outset, of course,
and from time to time the media would reveal in shocked tones that one band
or another didn't actually play on its records. Hedgehoppers Anonymous, the
Fortunes and Love Affair had all received negative publicity in this way, though
the practice extended much further: only Jim McGuinn contributed to the music
on the Byrds' 'Mr Tambourine Man', and Van Morrison's first band, Them, was
heavily augmented by outside musicians. But these were existing, real groups,
even if their producers didn't trust their competence in the studio. The first new
#1 of 1970 in Britain cut corners still further and revealed the industry's logical
development: the non-existent band.

Tony Burrows had been a minor figure in the British music scene for some
time, having sung with the Ivy League and the Flower Pot Men, but after ten years
on the road he had decided to give up playing gigs and to concentrate on studio
work. An initial spate of recordings all hit at the same time and he rapidly achieved
a rare domination of the top ten: in the last chart of February 1970 he was at #1
with 'Love Grows (Where My Rosemary Goes)', at #9 with 'My Baby Loves Loving'
and at #10 with 'United We Stand', these records being released under the names
Edison Lighthouse, White Plains and Brotherhood of Man respectively; he was also
featured that month on the Brotherhood of Man's hit 'United We Stand' and, a
couple of weeks later, on Pipkins' 'Gimme Dat Ding'. None of the alleged groups
existed outside the studio; all consisted simply of session players and singers. On
a single episode of *Top of the Pops*, Burrows appeared in three separate guises and
was promptly told that he was banned from the show because it was 'starting to
look like a bit of a fix'. He went on to appear on over a hundred hits during the
decade, but was seldom seen again on television.

Chairmen of the Board,
best known for the 1970 hit
'Give Me Just a Little More
Time'. From left to right:
Danny Woods, General
Johnson, Harrison Kennedy.

Johnny Johnson, whose group the Bandwagon were more successful in Britain than at home in America.

OPPOSITE: Gladys Knight, a former Motown star who turned to a softer soul sound in the 1970s with her band the Pips.

Martha Reeves and the Vandellas, whose 'Dancing in the Streets' was a bigger hit in Britain when reissued than it had been first time around.

Burrows wasn't the only one to arouse suspicions at *Top of the Pops*. Phil Wainman, before he became a successful producer, was a drummer in a variety of groups and was challenged by the show's producer: 'Weren't you here last week? And maybe even the week before?' Polly Brown, who had had hits as a member of Pickettywitch before going solo, also sang on a version of Abba's 'Honey Honey' under the name Sweet Dreams – so worried was she that she'd be recognized that, in the words of Ron Roker, the record's producer (and male singer), she 'turned up in a wig, calling herself Sierra Leone, and she'd put dark make-up on. She blacked up.' She was ordered to remove the make-up before appearing.

Even when the name on the record was familiar, it was no guarantee of personnel. American band the Drifters had been formed back in 1953 around former Dominoes singer Clyde McPhatter, and had been internationally successful for many years, but with an ever-shifting line-up, they began to lose direction in the late 1960s and were dropped by their American record label, Atlantic. Dick Leahy, the head of Bell Records in Britain, signed them and placed them in the hands of Roger Cook and Roger Greenaway. A new series of hits – mostly tame echoes of past glories – resulted, but the only authentic Drifter on them was veteran Johnny Moore, accompanied by the usual session musicians (Mike Moran was on piano, Chris Spedding on guitar) and with harmonies by, amongst others, the ubiquitous Tony Burrows: 'Roger Greenaway only used to let Johnny Moore sing on the records – the others took too long in the studio, so I used to sing on them.'

In such an environment, backing tracks became virtually indistinguishable, and there was always considerable leeway concerning whose name they would eventually emerge under: 'Some of those sessions from the Drifters ended up being Fortunes

LEFT: The Supremes and the Four Tops. From left to right: Obie Benson, Mary Wilson, Levi Stubbs, Jean Terrell, Duke Fakir, Cindy Birdsong, Lawrence Payton.

RIGHT: Dandy Livingstone, whose ska hits included 'Suzanne Beware of the Devil' and 'Rudy, A Message to You'.

BELOW: The Temptations: Dennis Edwards (front) with, from left to right, Richard Street, Otis Williams, Melvin Franklin, Damon Harris.

records,' recalled Spedding. There was the additional factor that, despite the professionalism of the players, these sessions never meant a great deal to them. 'As a studio-player, I exchange three hours of musical knowledge for cash; and beyond that I have no emotional involvement in it,' said bassist Herbie Flowers. 'I couldn't give a shit about the stuff. And it is only stuff.' The result was a chart that was increasingly uniform and bland, so that sales were driven down still further, as the public's enthusiasm continued to dissipate.

If this was a difficulty for *Top of the Pops*, as it certainly was, it was even more concerning to Radio One. And yet the station also contributed to the problem, entrenching the session acts. For it had been set up with the express intention of reflecting the charts, and had little inclination to look beyond. 'The management at Radio One were totally obsessed with singles,' noted Johnnie Walker, who had finally left Radio Caroline and been welcomed into the bosom of the BBC. 'The playlist for the daytime shows was made up of the current top 40, previous hit singles and a few new releases.' He fought for the inclusion on his show of album tracks but seldom with much success. And it wasn't the content of the music that raised objections but simply its non-single status; despite heavy lobbying, Walker wasn't allowed to play, for example, 'Layla' by Eric Clapton's latest group, Derek and the Dominoes, on its release in 1970, though two years later 'Radio One played it quite happily because it was a seven-inch single and made the charts – so it was now okay.' It was calculated in 1970 that just two per cent of the music played on Radio One's daytime shows came from outside the charts.

There was also a structural issue for the BBC that was difficult to overcome, as Bob Harris identified: 'Radio One was never going to be the same as the pirates. The BBC had draconian needle-time restrictions to adhere to.' The needle-time agreement was particularly inflexible, a deal reached many years earlier with the Musicians' Union, who insisted that only a certain amount of broadcasting time could be spent playing records, leaving opportunities for its members to play live or to record sessions for specific shows; the agreement allowed at this stage for just 50 hours a week of records across Radios One and Two, little more than three-and-a-half hours per day on each station. (The pirates simply hadn't bothered with such restrictions, which was why the Musicians' Union had campaigned so heavily against them.)

One option might have been to follow the model of the old Third Programme, now rebranded as Radio Three, and to turn Radio One into a largely live station, with daily concerts, but this doesn't seem to have been seriously considered. Instead the time that the station was on air was rationed to seven or eight hours

Mary Hopkin, whose single 'Those Were the Days' was the most successful record by another artist released on the Beatles' Apple label.

ABOVE LEFT: Cliff Richard, still a chart fixture in his third decade.

ABOVE RIGHT: David Cassidy, teen star of *The Partridge Family*.

OPPOSITE: The Drifters in their early 1970s incarnation, enjoying a new series of hits in Britain. Lead singer Johnny Moore (seated) joined the band in 1955.

a day, the remainder being shared with Radio Two. The shared airtime included plays, sitcoms and quizzes in the evening, as well as daytime shows that spread across both stations with veteran disc jockeys like Jimmy Young and Jack Johnson. What emerged from this arrangement, inevitably, was pop music of the lowest common denominator, with an emphasis on those records that weren't too raucous and couldn't possibly cause offence to an audience that encompassed all age ranges. In this world, the likes of Edison Lighthouse and the Drifters, with their unchallenging, singalong fare, were only too welcome.

There was an additional complication to Radio One's obsession with the charts: the fact that they didn't necessarily reflect public taste, owing to the long-standing practice known as hyping. 'There was a rumour', commented Brian Epstein of the Beatles' first single 'Love Me Do', 'that I had bought the disc in bulk to get it into the charts. Possible though this would have been – had I the money, which I hadn't – I did no such thing, nor ever have.' Others had fewer qualms. The number of shops that supplied sales information to the chart compilers was strictly limited at this stage, and once the list of the relevant outlets had been leaked, it wasn't difficult for sales to be arranged. 'This was comparatively easy,' admitted Simon Napier-Bell. 'You just phoned a guy called Gerry and told him what you wanted. He figured out how much money he could get out of you and told you that was the price. For instance, for a couple of hundred pounds he'd put you in around 29, or for a bit more you could go higher.'

OPPOSITE: The Equals, whose 1968 #1 'Baby Come Back' was followed by other hits, many of them written by guitarist Eddy Grant.

BELOW: The Herd, who continued after the departure of Peter Frampton. From left to right: Andy Bown, Gary Taylor, Henry Spinetti.

BELOW AND LEFT: The Jackson Five, the last of the classic Motown bands.

OVERLEAF: The Jackson Five. From left to right: Tito, Marlon, Michael, Jackie, Jermaine.

The Osmonds. From left to right: Merrill, Alan, Wayne, Jay with (seated) Donny.

For those who couldn't afford that service, the alternative was a do-it-yourself approach. Steve Thomas, later to become a successful designer, worked in the record industry in the mid 1960s and helped hype the first Herd hit, with the aid of a couple of assistants: 'Each of us would go into the record shops on the list, announce that we were the secretary of the Herd Fan Club and that we wanted to order 36 copies of the single. They didn't have that many copies in stock, of course, but they took our money, ordered the records and dutifully filled in the sales on their returns to be sent to the chart compilers in London.' He was successful enough that others began approaching him to do the same for them.

If all this paints a gloomy picture of British pop at the turn of the decade, then there were at least a couple of causes for cautious optimism. One was the prospect of competition from commercial radio, as promised by the Conservative Party back in 1967 when Radio One was first launched. The legislation was duly introduced and, despite the expected opposition from the Labour Party (their spokesman, Ivor Richards, insisted it would bring about the 'trivialization of broadcasting'), the first local commercial stations were launched in 1973. Admittedly, they largely followed the format of Radio One, but at least there were now alternatives, and there was the possibility of local tastes being reflected.

Even so, the best sounds in the British singles charts came from abroad, indirectly influenced by the mods' championing of dance music from Jamaica and Detroit some years earlier. On the one hand there was a fashion for the new Jamaican sounds of ska; sales of singles for Desmond Dekker, Bob and Marcia and Dandy Livingstone amongst others were driven by early skinheads, themselves descended from mod. And then there was a huge revival of interest in the Tamla Motown roster of artists. A series of compilation albums began to attract respectable sales, and in 1969 *Motown Chartbusters Volume 3* commenced what turned out to be a 93-week residency in the album charts, eventually reaching #1 early the following year. Similar success followed for *Volume 4* and *Volume 5*, and an accompanying series of reissued singles finally brought what had hitherto been a minority interest into the mainstream of British pop. In 1969 there were top five hits for Martha Reeves and the Vandellas' 'Dancing in the Streets' (five years earlier it had barely scraped into the top 30 and for the Temptations' 1966 classic 'Get Ready', which had flopped entirely. The following year saw top ten hits for the Four Tops with 'I Can't Help Myself' and Smokey Robinson and the Miracles with 'The Tracks of My Tears', both dating back to 1965. All of these sparked a new series of hits, sometimes – as was the case with the Vandellas – at a time when the band's American chart career had stalled.

This revival of early Motown, clearly caused in part by the flatness of current British pop, had two major effects. The first was the promotion of what became known as Northern Soul. Rooted in clubs such as the Twisted Wheel in Manchester and the Wigan Casino, this fiercely elitist scene celebrated old soul styles and, though it produced little original music in itself, it did help shape popular taste, most notably when 'Hey Girl Don't Bother Me' by the Tams, dating from 1964, became an unexpected British #1 in 1971. The second effect was to prepare the ground for the arrival in 1970 of the most popular Motown group of them all: the Jackson Five, fronted by the joyous pre-pubescent voice of Michael Jackson. They might not have been quite as huge in Britain as they were in America, but it was a close-run thing: their first four singles hit the top ten in the UK, while all went to #1 in the States.

ABOVE: Jimmy Savile and Micky Dolenz.

LEFT: Disc jockey Ed 'Stewpot' Stewart with members of the *Top of the Pops* audience.

Pan's People, the resident dance troupe on *Top of the Pops*, who tried to launch a singing career with the 1974 single 'You Can Really Rock and Roll Me'.

The success of the Jackson Five suggested that perhaps the days of the studio groups were numbered. Because there was an inherent flaw in the marketing of identikit records by session players, operating under random names: in the absence of a real group, prepared to go out on the road and build a following, they had a very limited shelf life. Edison Lighthouse's 'Love Grows' was a perfectly fine pop single, but there was no legion of fans holding its collective breath in eager anticipation of what the band might do next. In fact the follow-up, 'It's Up to You, Petula', spent just one week in the charts at #49. These records might be able to produce a speedy and lucrative return on their investment, but they had no longevity and ultimately the entire system was unsustainable.

What was needed for substantial, lasting success in the pop world was the kind of act Brian Epstein had identified back in 1964: 'those who are capable of having a kind of continuous folklore built up around them, so that the public wants to go on hearing *about* them, as well as hearing *from* them'. The huge success of the Jacksons demonstrated the truth of that assessment, as did the arrival of the Osmonds; marketed initially as a white alternative to the Five, and never receiving the praise lavished upon their rivals ('the Osmonds are not even phoney: they are sincerely vacuous,' wrote the *Observer*'s television critic Clive James), their various permutations managed to score thirteen hit singles in 1973 alone.

It was notable that this lesson came from America. There the whole cycle had been gone through already. The Monkees had been sold on their television series as a wacky but safe alternative to the Beatles, just as the originals were getting into drugs and being bigger than Jesus, but when they began publicly to voice their unhappiness at not being allowed to play on their own records, the industry concluded that an ever safer version was needed, one that wouldn't be able to rebel because it didn't exist. The result was the Archies, stars of an American animated television series – the music being created by session players – who scored the biggest international hit of 1969 with the bubblegum pop of 'Sugar Sugar', but, like Edison Lighthouse, couldn't retain the public's interest.

And so in 1970, two years after the last episode of *The Monkees* and one year after *The Brady Bunch* had first aired, ABC Television launched a kids' comedy-pop show, *The Partridge Family*, that spanned the two prototypes: the eponymous family were cosily middle-class and played in a band, both on-screen and off. Halfway through the first series, the group's debut single 'I Think I Love You' knocked the Jackson Five off the #1 position in America and, despite the group credit, it was abundantly clear to everyone that stardom was being conferred on David Cassidy, the best looking and most talented member of the family.

LEFT: Dana, who won the 1970 Eurovision Song Contest with 'All Kinds of Everything' and later became a Member of the European Parliament.

BELOW: The Three Degrees. From left to right: Fayette Pinkney, Valerie Holiday, Sheila Ferguson.

OVERLEAF: Karen Carpenter (left) and Lulu (right).

Gilbert O'Sullivan (left), Lynsey de Paul (centre) and Norman 'Hurricane' Smith (right).

The Partridge Family didn't arrive in Britain until a year later, but when it did, it was a colossal hit and Cassidy became the biggest scream star of the era, more popular even than Donny Osmond, for where the latter was reviving conventional songs of the pre-Beatles era ('Puppy Love', 'Too Young') in a perfectly phrased but ultimately saccharine style, Cassidy was making the doubt-ridden teen-angst of his material ('Could It Be Forever?', 'How Can I Be Sure?') sound as though he meant every word. So vast was the teen following he accrued that on his first visit to Britain in 1972, he was forbidden to appear on *Top of the Pops*, as Bill Cotton, head of BBC light entertainment, explained to Cassidy's label-boss Dick Leahy: 'He phoned me and explained why he was banning David Cassidy from the studio. He was worried about the security and worried about the thousands of people that followed David everywhere. If he booked him on the show, the whole place would be overrun by young fans.' The existence of such teen stars restored some of the excitement that the nation expected from its favourite pop show. Singles sales began to recover some lost ground, and *Top of the Pops*, after two years' absence, returned to the television top twenty.

Donny and David were the two most prominent American stars of 1972–74, evoking memories of the high-school pop purveyed by Bobby Vee, Bobby Vinton and Bobby Rydell in the days before the British invasion. But by then Britain too had woken up to the need to produce a new generation of musicians, one with the higher ambition of recreating the exhilaration of 1964.

OPPOSITE: Errol Brown of Hot Chocolate, one of the most successful chart bands of the 1970s.

ABOVE AND RIGHT: Love Affair, whose 'Everlasting Love' reached #1 in 1968. Above, from left to right: Mo Bacon, Morgan Fisher, Rex Brayley, Steve Ellis, Mick Jackson; right, Steve Ellis, one of the most underrated R&B singers of the era, performing their later hit 'One Road'.

chapter seven

YOU WEAR IT WELL

Writing in 1969, the critic George Melly observed that 'British pop music is teetering on the edge of becoming art,' and went on to predict that rock and roll would follow the model of jazz and 'become a minority interest'. He was, of course, referring primarily to the album-based bands, but his predictions were mistaken. The split between albums and singles, between rock and pop, was to be resolved by a new wave of acts, who set their sights on having it all: critically acclaimed albums, a near-residency on *Top of the Pops* and good old-fashioned stardom. Equally at home in the rock weeklies and in teen magazines, they were led initially by Marc Bolan's band T.Rex, who in 1971, after eight consecutive victories for the Beatles, were voted the Best UK Vocal Group by the readers of the *New Musical Express* in their annual poll; so influential did Bolan prove to be that he launched a genre – glam rock – that was swiftly populated by a host of others.

It started with T.Rex's 'Ride a White Swan' at the end of 1970, picked up speed with Slade's breakthrough the following year, and then really took off in the summer of 1972, with hits for David Bowie, Gary Glitter, Roxy Music and Mott the Hoople. These market leaders were joined by existing acts finding their own take on this new style: bubblegum pop band the Sweet; Wizzard, based around Roy Wood, veteran of the Move and the Electric Light Orchestra; Alvin Stardust, who had been moderately successful in pre-Beatles days as Shane Fenton. And although primarily a British phenomenon, there was room too for certain American acts, with Alice Cooper and Lou Reed heading the field.

Glam was from the outset as unstable an alliance as the beat boom had been. There was little in the music itself to bind together, say, the arthouse ambition of Roxy Music with the stomping riffs of Gary Glitter, but what linked all the acts

OPPOSITE: Marc Bolan.

OPPOSITE: Mungo Jerry. From left to right: Colin Earl, Mike Cole, Ray Dorset, Paul King.

was an attitude towards showmanship that was born of frustration with the existing order of dressed-down electric blues bands. 'Things got indulgent, that's what happened. People were wearing duller clothes or denims and they were looking at the floor. They were all post-hippies, you see, hadn't quite recovered from the drugs,' explained Dave Hill, guitarist with Slade. 'Rock seemed to have wandered into some kind of denim hell,' agreed Bowie; 'rather dull attitudinizing with none of the burning ideals of the Sixties.'

Indeed many of the glam stars were survivors from the mod days of the mid 1960s. 'I remember Marc Bolan with full make-up on working as a rent boy to buy clothes, in and around the Scene Club,' said Pete Townshend. 'He was about fifteen.' Bolan's own memory, albeit with a couple of years knocked off his age, put him in the same place: 'When I was thirteen I was really into clothes as an energy force – the same way that I'm now into music,' he said in 1972, at the height of his fame. Bowie too had been hanging around the London scene: 'I've always worn make-up,' he pointed out. 'I first began to fool around with it years ago when I was a mod. I was a very heavy mod, and I used to wear ankle swingers and luminous socks.' Gary Glitter, meanwhile, had done a long stint as the warm-up act on *Ready Steady Go!*

Dave Edmunds, who had some success with Love Sculpture before 'I Hear You Knocking' launched a solo career.

Those glam stars who came from outside the charmed inner circles of London had likewise been keeping the faith. 'There's a photograph of me taken in '67 which is quite interesting to compare with some psychedelic pictures of contemporaries,' noted Bryan Ferry of Roxy Music. 'I never went through [psychedelia] at all. I'm wearing a midnight blue mohair suit, with a button-down collar shirt, posing against a Studebaker. I was much more flash then than I am now.' And even Slade, seemingly a more straightforward proposition, had long been busy pursuing the mods' favourite music: 'We were doing Motown when it was considered underground,' insisted bass guitarist Jim Lea.

The result was that glam bore many of the hallmarks of the original mod ethos: an obsession with clothes and image, a devotion to dancing, an awareness

Marc Bolan, the first glam rock star.

of the power of the seven-inch single. There was also the association with Pop Art, now taken a stage further so that the glam stars no longer merely celebrated idols of pop culture, but sought self-consciously to make idols of themselves. 'People are really works of art, and if you have a nice face you might as well play about with it,' said Bolan. 'The fabric of my work is using my body, my personality as well as my songs and stage performance,' Bowie explained later in his career, 'rather like a canvas.' So when Bowie launched the character of Ziggy Stardust with *The Rise and Fall of Ziggy Stardust and the Spiders from Mars* (1972), it was not so much a concept album as conceptual art, a project that was lived out by Bowie himself in person; 'like a portrait in flesh,' as he sang on 'Sweet Thing'.

The tendency towards self-glorification was immediately noticeable on album covers. Where the biggest bands of the era – Pink Floyd, Led Zeppelin, ELP – went for allusive, indirect imagery, downplaying

RIGHT: T.Rex. From left to right: Steve Currie, Marc Bolan, Mickey Finn, Bill Legend.

OVERLEAF: Slade at Belle Vue, Manchester. From left to right: Don Powell, Dave Hill, Noddy Holder, Jim Lea; and (right) Noddy Holder on *Top of the Pops*.

The Alice Cooper band. Clockwise from left: Glen Buxton, Dennis Dunaway, Michael Bruce, Neal Smith, Alice Cooper.

even the name of the group, glam acts put themselves proudly on the sleeve; every Bowie album jacket throughout his career has featured his image. Virtually the only exception was Roxy Music: Bryan Ferry, having studied under Richard Hamilton at art school, had an affection for the airbrushed gloss of advertising and used fantasy images of models, shot by fashion photographer Karl Stoecker.

The mod heritage was a key element in glam, but so too was the rock and roll revival that had surfaced seriously in 1969. The following year two #1 singles in Britain broke that revival into the mainstream: Dave Edmunds' cover of 'I Hear You Knocking' and Mungo Jerry's 'In the Summertime'. The latter, a quasi-skiffle shuffle with such an exuberant sense of fun that it became an international hit, was a clear influence on Bolan. Growing disenchanted with achieving nothing more than cult status (inevitable given his childlike acoustic songs about a 'world of unicorns and gypsy elves'), he now took up an electric guitar for the first glam hit, 'Ride a White Swan', a record that could have been – and in some quarters

PREVIOUS PAGES: David Bowie with guitarist Mick Ronson, performing 'Starman' on *Top of the Pops*.

OPPOSITE: Gary Glitter, a veteran of the early rock and roll scene, who finally became a star in 1972 with the instrumental 'Rock and Roll (Part 2)'.

actually was – mistaken for Mungo Jerry. 'Marc Bolan said that he had similar roots to myself, because he was interested in the old rockabilly stuff, and Leadbelly and all that,' remembered sideburn-clad singer Ray Dorset of Mungo Jerry. 'And he said that when "In the Summertime" became such a big hit, he realized you could have a hit pop song with a 12-bar. Well, people had been doing that for years, anyway.'

For glam, the return of rock and roll was grist to the mill, absorbed along with a host of other influences, from Berlin cabaret to science fiction to Dylanesque wordplay. Certainly it informed the music, restoring a directness and brevity that had seemed lost. 'I'd been in the wings during a Little Richard concert in Berlin,' Gary Glitter said, explaining the genesis of his new sound, 'and realized that rock and roll was what I should be doing.' More than simply the sounds, though, the revival fed into the iconography of glam. 'I saw the songs in the context of Pop Art,' said Brian Eno of Roxy Music. 'That was the period when pop music became sort of self-conscious, in the sense that it started to look at its own history as material that could be used.'

Mott the Hoople. From left to right: Verden Allen, Dale Griffin, Mick Ralphs, Overend Watts, Ian Hunter.

RIGHT: The Sweet backstage in costume for their 1972 'Wig-Wam Bam'.

LEFT: The Sweet performing 'Wig-Wam Bam' on *Top of the Pops*. From left to right: Mick Tucker, Steve Priest, Andy Scott, Brian Connolly.

One manifestation of this plundering of the past was the ubiquity of the phrase itself, from Gary Glitter's first hit 'Rock and Roll (Parts 1 & 2)' and Wizzard's 'Rock 'n' Roll Winter' to David Bowie's 'Rock 'n' Roll with Me' and even the Rolling Stones' 'It's Only Rock and Roll'. Another was the adoption of stage names, which had been standard practice in the 1950s but had been largely absent from British rock in the 1960s (with the exception of Ringo Starr); by contrast, Bolan and Bowie used invented names as did, more obviously, Gary Glitter and Alvin Stardust. There was a celebration of artifice, in deliberate opposition to the drive for authenticity evident elsewhere.

The artifice was most evident, of course, in the make-up and the clothes. Bolan began with relatively uncontroversial clothes, albeit accessorized with a

feather boa and with glittery cosmetics, but Bowie had been photographed wearing a dress designed by Mr Fish for the cover of his 1971 album *The Man Who Sold the World*, and the idea of dressing-up became the defining feature of glam. 'The first time I ever saw Bowie wearing make-up was on John Peel's show,' remembered his bassist, Trevor Bolder. 'I'd seen him in jeans and t-shirt, and all of a sudden this guy comes out wearing a bloody dress, covered in make-up. And it was a radio show. So no one was going to see him.'

Amongst those most committed to the dressing-up box was Dave Hill of Slade: 'What I wore on *Top of the Pops* on our first hit record, which was "Get Down And Get With It", was a pink woman's coat. I had diamonds on my dungarees, under the pink coat, into my boots.' He then bought a long black coat and sprayed it silver: 'The silver coat used to work great on a black and white TV,

OPPOSITE: Roy Wood, formerly of the Move and Electric Light Orchestra, reborn as a glam star with Wizzard.

10cc. From left to right: Eric Stewart, Lol Creme, Kevin Godley, Graham Gouldman.

223

BELOW AND OPPOSITE:
Elton John, the biggest star
to come out of Britain in
the 1970s.

because people didn't need colour to see it, it would reflect,' he reasoned, this being a time when only twelve per cent of British households had colour television. The concern with television was important, for glam exhibited none of the disdain for the medium seen in other quarters – Led Zeppelin, for example, made no appearances at all on British television in their heyday. 'Glam rock was all about putting on a spectacle,' said Mike Leander, who had worked as arranger on records for Marianne Faithfull and the Beatles ('She's Leaving Home') before going on to co-write and produce Gary Glitter's hits. 'The records, too, were constructed to be seen, whereas in the late Sixties they were constructed to be heard, preferably with a joint dangling from your mouth.'

Although artists like Bowie and Roxy Music were challenging the critics' dismissal of hit singles, a distinction was still being drawn between them on the one side and the more straightforwardly pop acts on the other. And one of the key issues was the control exercised by producers and writers. The Sweet were particularly affected, their hits being written by a new team of Nicky Chinn and Mike Chapman. The early singles ('Funny Funny', 'Co-Co') were pure bubblegum, seeking to emulate the Archies, and as such were created by session musicians, as their producer Phil Wainman happily acknowledged: 'I played on them because time was money and studio time was expensive even in those days.' The band themselves contributed vocals, but grew increasingly embittered with the process, demanding the right to be allowed to play on their own records. In 1972 they finally got their wish and 'Wig-Wam Bam' was their own performance, even if the song itself (a playground retelling of Henry Wadsworth Longfellow's 'The Song of Hiawatha') wasn't, and even if the *Top of the Pops* presentation was hardly likely to see them being taken more seriously.

The Sweet continued to rely on Chinn and Chapman for another two-and-a-half years, becoming ever more demanding of their writers. Given a demo for a new song 'Dyna-Mite' in 1973, they rejected it and demanded a substitute; instead the song was handed to another band, Mud, who took it into the top five. Nonetheless, this wasn't just a continuation of the interchangeable groups policy

OVERLEAF: The Faces. From
left to right: Ronnie Lane,
Ian McLagan, Rod Stewart,
Ron Wood, Kenny Jones.

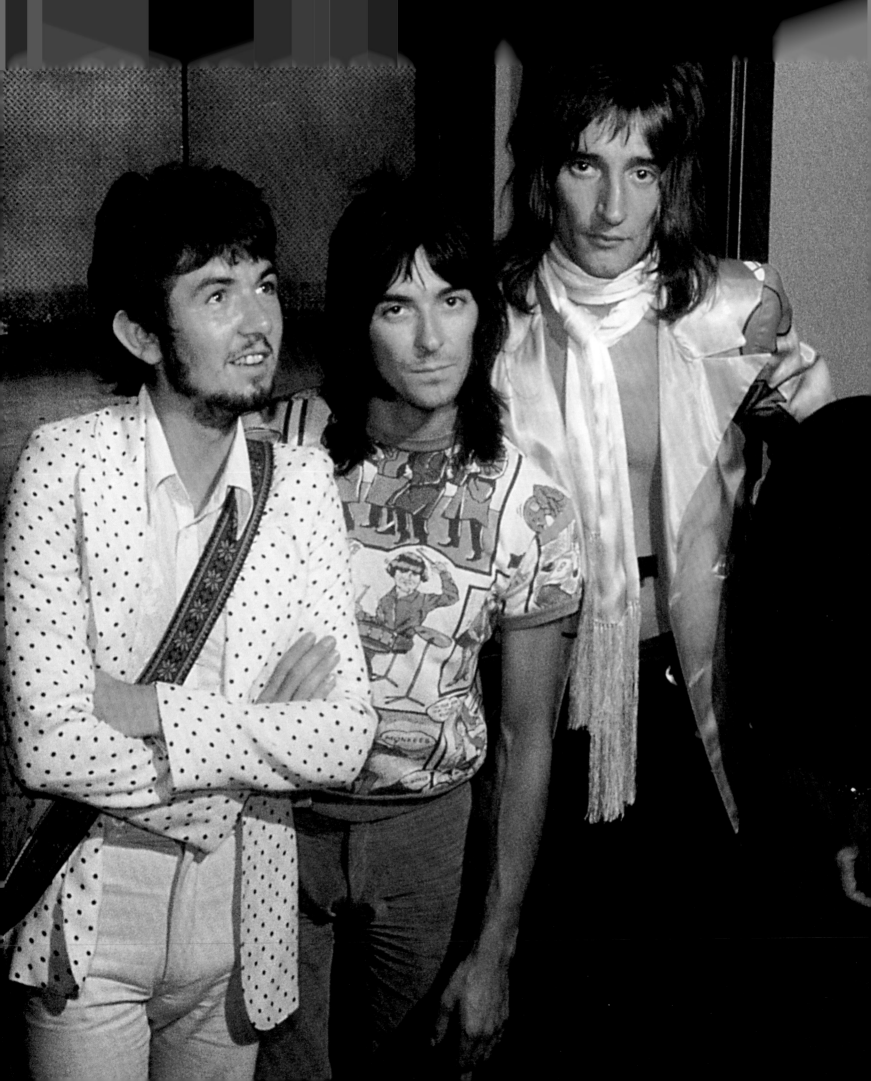

favoured by Cook and Greenaway; for the most part, the Chinn and Chapman records did actually sound different to each other: 'They tailored whatever they wrote,' insisted Suzi Quatro, another of their acts; 'they wrote for me.' But the stigma of playing material written by outsiders continued, especially as the Chinn and Chapman empire grew in power. In 1974 they sold more singles in Britain than the Beatles had managed in any one year, and that February – as the nation headed for the polling booths to remove Edward Heath's government, amidst power cuts, a fuel crisis and the misery of the three-day week – they held three of the top four positions in the charts, with Mud's 'Tiger Feet', Suzi Quatro's 'Devil Gate Drive' and the Sweet's 'Teenage Rampage'.

The domination of Chinn and Chapman had the effect of driving away from glam its more self-assured artists, most notably – in the cases of Bowie and Roxy Music – into an embrace of disco. But in any event, the music had already run its course; by the end of 1974 it was effectively all over, and those who didn't adapt faded away, with Slade, who had been touted at one stage as the new Beatles, being amongst those who lost their way. Dave Hill remembered the disc jockey Alan Freeman asking them when they were going to do their *Sgt Pepper*, but had to admit: 'Unfortunately we hadn't got songs about pilchards climbing up the Eiffel Tower. We hadn't moved into that one.'

ABOVE LEFT: Mud. Clockwise from left: Ray Stiles, Rob Davies, Dave Mount, Les Grey.

ABOVE RIGHT: The Rubettes. From left to right: Tony Thorpe, Mick Clarke, Alan Williams, Bill Hurd, John Richardson.

OPPOSITE: Alvin Stardust, who had his first hit in 1961 under the name Shane Fenton.

229

At its height, glam had been capable of seducing a mainstream performer like Elton John. A fringe figure from the London R&B scene, he had played in Long John Baldry's group, Bluesology (where he 'looked the image of the boy who played Piggy in the film *Lord of the Flies*', according to the band's backing singer Marsha Hunt), and had since turned himself into a singer-songwriter to great acclaim. Nonetheless he gleefully joined in, not only donning sillier costumes than anyone else, but having hits with 'Honky Cat', 'Crocodile Rock' and 'Saturday Night's Alright for Fighting', which were glam in all but spirit. He too drifted away musically in 1974, though the dressing-up continued.

Others had been less convinced and pursued a different course throughout. Most successful of all was Rod Stewart, another former mod but one without the higher artistic pretensions. Linking up with what remained of the Small Faces after Steve Marriott's departure, he became singer with the Faces and, both in that capacity and as a solo artist, he rivalled the glam acts at home and easily eclipsed them in America; with 'Maggie May' and *Every Picture Tells a Story*, he became the first act to be at #1 in the singles and albums charts in both Britain and America simultaneously. He and the Faces did so with a blend of straight rock, balladry and country-soul that fitted in with nothing else much in Britain at the time.

Equally out on a limb were 10cc, a Manchester band that included Eric Stewart, formerly of Wayne Fontana and the Mindbenders, and Graham Gouldman, whose songwriting had produced hits for the Yardbirds, the Hollies and Herman's Hermits. Signed by Jonathan King to his UK label and named by him, they pursued a wilfully individual route of witty, intelligent pop that owed little to anyone. They had, however, in an earlier guise as Hotlegs, produced a 1970 single, 'Neanderthal Man', that pre-empted the monolithic rhythms of glam.

Despite the continuing success of these acts, the decline of glam, and concurrently of Donny Osmond and David Cassidy, again left a vacuum in the singles charts. And again it was the inheritors of the Tin Pan Alley tradition that surfaced. The second wave of glam pop acts eased themselves into a more blatant recreation of pre-Beatles music with Mud's Elvis-impersonating 'Lonely this Christmas' and Alvin Stardust's 'Good Love Can Never Die', cementing a trend that had already begun earlier in 1974. The team of Wayne Bickerton and Tony Waddington, for example, had written a song, 'Sugar Baby Love', that was rooted in white doo-wop and was aimed at the Eurovision Song Contest; when it failed to be selected as Britain's entry, they recorded it with session players, put it out under the name the Rubettes and watched it sell millions of copies all over Europe. Unusually, in this instance the studio musicians chose to become also the public group.

The Bay City Rollers.
Clockwise from top left:
Derek Longmuir,
Les McKeown, John Devine,
Alan Longmuir, Eric Faulkner.

Elton John (left), Marc Bolan (centre) and Rod Stewart (right).

The band that really prospered, though, in the twilight of glam were the Bay City Rollers. They had had a hit in 1971 under the stewardship of Jonathan King, but then disappeared before coming back in 1974 with a string of lightweight, summer hits written and produced by Bill Martin and Phil Coulter. The music was played by a familiar team of session men with the Rollers only contributing vocals, and – like the Sweet before them – the band grew restless; they moved from Martin and Coulter and struck out on their own for their biggest British hit, a revival of the Four Seasons' 'Bye Bye Baby'.

When the rock and roll revival in 1968–70 had turned back the clock, it had sought inspiration in the first generation of rockers: the rebellious imagery of Elvis Presley, Jerry Lee Lewis and Little Richard. Now, a few years later, the influences too had moved on a few years, to the more anodyne American pop of the Kennedy era just before the Beatles revolutionized the industry.

By 1975, then, it felt as though British rock and roll had come round to the end of a cycle. The initial burst of activity that had seen the emergence of the Beatles, the Rolling Stones and the Who, had unravelled once already towards the end of the 1960s, the flash and excitement dissipated. It had then enjoyed a new lease of life with glam – fronted by former mods – and had again come to a halt. One might have concluded that the future belonged to disco and to airbrushed stadium superstars, rather than to the noisy but arty guitar groups that had been Britain's greatest contribution to rock and roll. And even though that turned out not to be the case, it would have been an honest mistake: the immediate signs were not encouraging.

What hadn't changed was *Top of the Pops*. After its initial years in Manchester, it had relocated to London, but the format remained essentially the same, with the basic rules laid down by Johnnie Stewart at the outset still in place – only records going up the charts, no record to appear two weeks in succession unless it was at #1. Now an institution, a fixture in the television schedules and in the weekly rhythm of millions of families, it had transcended its source material and was seemingly impervious to all changes in the music. In 1975, a far from vintage year in British rock and roll, it finally broke into the top five of the television charts for the first time. The great demographic bulge that had peaked in 1964, the only year in which the British birth rate exceeded one million, was reaching adolescence and *Top of the Pops* was extending its influence to a new generation.

'Somebody asked me on the first show, "How long do you think this will last for?",' remembered Jimmy Savile. 'I said, "As long as people buy records, because they will love seeing the artist on telly." And I was dead right.'

References

Some of the material in the text derives from personal conversations or correspondence. Below is a list of references for material that has been quoted from published sources. Publication details of books are given in the bibliography.

Introduction: Top of the Pop Photographers
The quotes in this chapter are taken from personal interviews, from an article by Terry Christian in *The Times* 31/5/2008 and from the 2005 BBC TV documentary *Harry Goodwin: Shooting Stars*.

Chapter one: Ferry Across the Mersey
'The beat scene' – Robb, *The North Will Rise Again* p.9; 'It was stuck on top' – Cohn, *Awopbopaloobop Alopbambloom* pp.163–4; 'late-night ghetto television' – Carpenter, *That Was Satire that Was* p.215; 'We had the same timing' – *ibid.* p.219; 'Our young men and women' – Wilson, *The New Britain* p.10; 'lamb dressed as mutton' – *Punch*, 21/9/1983; 'Young people are the trendsetters' – Everett, *You'll Never Be 16 Again* p.67; 'Suddenly people from Liverpool' – Oldham, *Stoned* p.298; 'We've always *hated* him' – Kureishi & Savage, *The Faber Book of Pop* p.191; 'simultaneously omniscient' – Oldham *op. cit.* p.172; 'People said their image' – Napier-Bell, *You Don't Have to Say You Love Me* p.96; 'It seems to me that these blokes' – *The Times* 26/2/1964; 'Like it or lump it' – *The Times* 19/12/1963; 'They put together' – Unterberer, *Turn! Turn! Turn!* p.63; 'British domination of Broadway' – Booker, *The Neophiliacs* p.231; 'life in England' – Mortimer, *Paradise Postponed* pp.142–3; 'Just about everyone' – Clayson, *The Beat Merchants* p.186; 'the huge faces' – Kureishi & Savage *op. cit.* pp.197–8; '*Ready Steady Go!* was doing amazing things' – Blacknell, *The Story of Top of the Pops* p.16; 'Mr Wilson is and always has been' – *The Times* 28/9/1963; 'If you want to see who's in the top twenty' – *NME* 6/11/71; 'P.J. Proby gets pawed' – Mabey, *The Pop Process* p.126; 'fascinatingly dreadful' – Melly, *Revolt Into Style* p.190; 'That man is box office' – Blacknell *op. cit.* p.20; 'The crew were tripping over each other' – Gittins, *Top of the Pops* p.9; 'I remember screaming' – Everett *op. cit.* p.49; 'My mother watched' – Rhys Jones, *Semi-Detached* p.172; 'We loved doing *Top of the Pops*' – Gittins *op. cit.* p.12; 'Like everybody else of my generation' – Rossi & Parfitt, *XS All Areas* p.107.

Chapter two: Yeh Yeh
'Everything was special' – Essex, *A Charmed Life* p.27; 'One didn't only dress up for girls' – Freeman, *The Leather Boys* p.26; 'Girls were out of fashion' – Everett, *You'll Never Be 16 Again* p.56; 'The whole mod thing' – Oldham, *Stoned* p.220; 'They were true dandies' – Melly, *Revolt Into Style* p.150; 'We hope to stay smart for ever' – Hillier, *The Style of the Century* p.173; 'It swings; it is the scene' – *Time* 15/4/1966; 'There's quite a crisis' – Mabey, *The Pop Process* p.84; 'turnover-worship' – Levin, *The Pendulum Years* p.185; 'It wasn't some great idea we had' – Oldham *op. cit.* p.342; 'was the most gorgeous chap' – *Guardian* 30/11/1999; 'A mod programme' – Fletcher, *Quadrophenia* p.55; 'She was awfully gauche' – Kingsley & Tibballs, *Box of Delights* p.72; '*Ready Steady Go!* was the showcase' – Turner, *The Biba Experience* p.16; 'For girls, looking deliberately dowdy' – Kingsley & Tibballs *op. cit.* p.72; 'Before us, groups were popular first' – Smith, *Off the Record* p.217; 'The British are not an artistic race' – Crisp, *Resident Alien* p.28; 'Pop Art borrowed from real pop' – Melly *op. cit.* p.104; 'which had a whole room full' – Green, *Days in the Life* p.63; 'I wanted to be in the presence' – Clayson, *The Beat Merchants* p.190; 'a wonderful scene' – *Mojo* issue 184, March 2009; 'When we came down to London' – Green *op. cit.* pp.46–7; 'England has such a small show business community' – Smith *op. cit.* p.207; 'He learns to tap-dance' – Kureishi & Savage, *The Faber Book of Pop* p.189; 'In a small society' – Connolly, *Stardust Memories* p.25; 'as if Pop Art had discovered Chekhov' – *Mojo* issue 184, March 2009; 'I feel that when people like the Beatles' – *The Times* 15/6/1965; 'The reaction was wholly unfavourable' – Castle, *The Castle Diaries* p.21; 'Some other decoration' – Kureishi & Savage, *op. cit.* p.238; 'The plain truth is' – Benn, *Out of the Wilderness* p.273; 'When the Beatles got the MBE' – Kingsley & Tibballs *op. cit.* p.72; 'The theatre started going downhill' – Orton, *The Orton Diaries* p.74; 'They were regarded as clean-living lads' – *The Sunday Times* 27/2/1982; 'brushed him aside, saying' – Dalton, *The Rolling Stones* p.57.

Chapter three: Catch the Wind
'a voice like sand and glue' – David Bowie, 'Song for Bob Dylan' (MainMan/Chrysalis, 1972); 'They were doing things' – Scaduto, *Bob Dylan* p.175; 'It's fucking *wild*' – *ibid.* p.176; 'I don't want to be interviewed' – *Disc* 22/5/1965; 'I suppose it will be controversial' – *NME*

24/9/1965; 'ROCK 'N' ROLL SONG BECOMING' – Unterberer, *Turn! Turn! Turn!* p.172; 'we achieved nothing' – Denselow, *When the Music's Over* p.93; 'America was still boss' – Whitcomb, *After the Ball* p.259.

Chapter four: Purple Haze

'We're more popular than Jesus' – *Evening Standard* 4/3/1966; 'The Beatles are not welcome in Memphis', 'The Beatles will not, by word' and 'We think of it every day' – Kureishi & Savage, *The Faber Book of Pop* pp.278–283; 'Secunda can stand as the most perfect specimen' – Melly, *Revolt Into Style* p.105; 'The prime minister has, in fact, for some years' – *The Times* 12/10/1967; 'I suppose you could say' – Owen, *Time to Declare* p.687; 'We've never had time before' – *Evening Standard* 4/3/1966; 'I get bored like anyone else' – Connolly, *Stardust Memories* p.37; 'Nothing could disguise the fact' – *Evening Standard* 29/12/1966; 'All them hard bad-trip records' – Green, *Days in the Life* p.83; 'Scandinavian boutiques are already' – *Encounter* October 1967; 'The underground was terribly small' – Green *op. cit.* p.187; 'like cries of dying galaxies' – *Private Eye: Private Pop Eye*; 'When I was drinking' – Burdon/Briggs/Weider/Jenkins/McCulloch, 'Good Times' (Sealark Ent/Slamina Music, 1967); 'LSD came along and the music' – *All My Loving* BBC documentary (1968); 'They were down on Herman's Hermits' – Smith, *Off the Record* p.212; 'It changed a lot of good blokes' – *Melody Maker* 11/11/1967; 'designed to take the mickey out of' – *Bucketfull of Brains* issue 4, 1982; 'I didn't even know how to spell psychedelic' – Rossi & Parfitt, *XS All Areas* p.77; 'None of us were drug-mad' – Buckley & Ellingham, *The Rough Guide to Rock* p.911; 'individuals of exaggerated dress' – Haslam, *Manchester, England* p.101; 'These clubs naturally attract the young' – *Hansard* 3/2/1967; 'There is a tendency to decry youth' – Everett, *You'll Never Be 16 Again* p.64; 'rather see a young man' – Symons, *Bloody Murder* p.44; 'No matter how many raids' – Everett, *op. cit.* p.74; 'the music business had changed for good' – Napier-Bell, *You Don't Have to Say You Love Me* p.109; 'Pop music seems to be splitting in two' – Harris, *The Whispering Years* p.26.

Chapter five: Won't Get Fooled Again

'culture-free programmes' – Whitcomb, *After the Ball* p.170; 'References, jokes or songs' – Mabey, *The Pop Process* p.117; 'convinced that if hit records' – Walker, *The Autobiography* p.142; 'legislation was at an advanced stage' – Benn, *Out of the Wilderness* pp.162–3; 'I have tried to get a pirate Bill' – *ibid.* p.415; 'Gangsterism has moved into' – *ibid.* p.437; 'One has to be wary' – Henry & Joel, *Pirate*

Radio p.72; 'Taking a trip' – *The Times* 16/7/1966; 'part of a revolution' – Everett, *You'll Never Be 16 Again* p.62; 'a flower-powered swinging chick' – Mabey *op. cit.* p.115; 'I don't want to be a clown anymore' – Kureishi & Savage, *The Faber Book of Pop* p.346; 'It's a terrible song' – Denselow, *When the Music's Over* p.97; 'The first Tory leader' – Booker, *The Neophiliacs* pp.27–8; 'It is a little known fact' – Henry & Joel *op. cit.* p.27; 'because there is an increasing number' – Tony Palmer interview, *All My Loving* DVD (2007); 'It is not for me to inflict' – *Times* 16/11/1968; 'It said more about pop' – Melly, *Revolt Into Style* p.182; '*Top of the Pops* was the singles show' – Harris, *The Whispering Years* p.106; 'I thought *Top of the Pops* was encouraging the yob culture' – Croft, *You Have Been Watching* p.189; 'The Small Faces' whole scene' – Pascall, *The Story of Pop* p.450; 'fuck off' – *Independent* 4/5/2005; 'had come to the position' – Green, *Days in the Life* p.292; 'Looking back, I don't think it was a good idea' – Connolly, *Stardust Memories* p.77.

Chapter six: Those Were the Days

'The management at Radio One' – Walker, *The Autobiography* p.166; 'Radio One played it quite happily' – *ibid.* p.145; 'Radio One was never going to be the same'– Harris, *The Whispering Years* p.37; 'There was a rumour' – Kureishi & Savage, *The Faber Book of Pop* p.185; 'This was comparatively easy' – Napier-Bell, *You Don't Have to Say You Love Me* p.65; 'trivialization of broadcasting' – *Daily Mail* 12/11/1971; 'those who are capable' – *Observer* 17/5/1964; 'the Osmonds are not even phoney' – James, *The Crystal Bucket* p.90; 'He phoned me and explained' – Cassidy, *Could It Be Forever?* p.131.

Chapter seven: You Wear It Well

'British pop music is teetering' – Melly, *Revolt Into Style* p.121; 'Rock seemed to have wandered' – Rock & Bowie, *Moonage Daydream* p.11; 'I remember Marc Bolan' – Oldham, *Stoned* p.220; 'When I was thirteen' – Connolly, *Stardust Memories* p.171; 'I've always worn make-up' – *ibid.* p.190; 'There's a photograph of me' – *Melody Maker* 6/7/1974; 'People are really works of art' – Hoskyns, *Glam!* p.22; 'The fabric of my work' – Buckley, *Strange Fascination* p.139; 'world of unicorns' – Hunt, *Real Life* p.120; 'I'd been in the wings during a Little Richard' – *Times* 29/11/1973; 'I saw the songs' – Hoskyns *op. cit.* p.58; 'Glam rock was all about' – *Mojo* issue 47, October 1997; 'looked the image of the boy who played Piggy' – Hunt *op. cit.* p.102; 'Somebody asked me' – Gittins, *Top of the Pops* p.9.

Bibliography

Note: Where a paperback or revised edition is shown, it indicates that any page numbers in the references are from that edition.

Tony Benn, *Out of the Wilderness: Diaries 1963–67* (Hutchinson, 1987; pbk edn: Arrow, 1988)

Steve Blacknell, *The Story of Top of the Pops* (Patrick Stephens, 1985)

Christopher Booker, *The Neophiliacs: A Study of the Revolution in English Life in the Fifties and Sixties* (Collins, 1969; pbk edn: Fontana, 1970)

David Buckley, *Strange Fascination: David Bowie – The Definitive Story* (Virgin Books, 1999; rev pbk edn: 2005)

Jonathan Buckley & Mark Ellingham (ed.), *The Rough Guide to Rock* (Rough Guides, 1996)

Humphrey Carpenter, *That Was Satire That Was: Beyond the Fringe, The Establishment Club, Private Eye and That Was the Week That Was* (Victor Gollancz, 2000)

David Cassidy, *Could It Be Forever? My Story* (Headline, 2007)

Barbara Castle, *The Castle Diaries 1964–1976* (Papermac, 1990)

Alan Clayson, *The Beat Merchants: The Origins, History, Impact and Rock Legacy of the 1960s British Pop Groups* (Blandford, 1995)

Nik Cohn, *Awopbopaloobop Alopbamboom: Pop from the Beginning* (Weidenfeld & Nicolson, 1969; pbk edn: Paladin, 1970)

Ray Connolly, *Stardust Memories: Talking about my Generation* (Pavilion, 1983)

Roger Crimlis & Alwyn W. Turner, *Cult Rock Posters 1972–1982: From Boys in Drag to Buffalo Gals* (Aurum, 2006)

Quentin Crisp, *Resident Alien: The New York Diaries* (HarperCollins, 1996)

David Croft, *You Have Been Watching ... The Autobiography* (BBC, 2004)

David Dalton (ed.), *The Rolling Stones: The Greatest Rock 'n' Roll Band in the World* (Star, 1975)

A.J. Davies, *To Build a New Jerusalem: The Labour Movement from the 1880s to the 1990s* (Michael Joseph, 1992)

Robin Denselow, *When the Music's Over: The Story of Political Pop* (rev edn: Faber & Faber, 1990)

David Essex, *A Charmed Life: The Autobiography* (Orion, 2002)

Peter Everett, *You'll Never Be 16 Again: An Illustrated History of the British Teenager* (BBC, 1986)

Paul Ferris, *Sir Huge: The Life of Huw Wheldon* (Michael Joseph, 1990)

Paul Ferris, *Sex and the British: A Twentieth Century History* (Michael Joseph, 1993)

Alan Fletcher, *Quadrophenia* (Corgi, 1979)

Jim Fowler, *Unleashing Britain: Theatre Gets Real 1955–64* (V&A Publications, 2005)

Gillian Freeman, *The Leather Boys* (Anthony Blond, 1961, under the pseudonym Eliot George; pbk edn: New English Library, 1969)

Paul Gambaccini, Tim Rice & Jonathan Rice, *British Hit Albums* (Guinness Publishing, 1983; 5th edition, 1992)

Charlie Gillett, *The Sound of the City: The Rise of Rock and Roll* (Souvenir, 1970; rev edn: 1983)

Ian Gittins, *Top of the Pops: Mishaps, Miming and Music – True Adventures of TV's No.1 Pop Show* (BBC, 2007)

Jonathan Green, *Days in the Life: Voices from the English Underground 1961–1971* (William Heinemann, 1988; pbk edn: Pimlico, 1998)

Dave Harker, *One for the Money: Politics and Popular Song* (Hutchinson, 1980)

Bob Harris, *The Whispering Years* (BBC Worldwide, 2001)

Dave Haslam, *Manchester, England: The Story of the Pop Cult City* (Fourth Estate, 1999)

Stuart Henry & Mike von Joel, *Pirate Radio: Then and Now* (Blandford Press, 1984)

Bevis Hillier, *The Style of the Century* (Herbert Press, 1983; rev. edn: 1998)

Barney Hoskyns, *Glam! Bowie, Bolan and the Glitter Rock Revolution* (Faber & Faber, 1998)

Marsha Hunt, *Real Life* (Chatto & Windus, 1986)

Lesley Jackson, *The Sixties: Decade of Design Revolution* (Phaidon, 1998)

Clive James, *The Crystal Bucket* (Picador, 1981)

Tony Jasper (ed.), *British Record Charts 1955–1979* (Futura, 1979)

Hanif Kureishi & Jon Savage (ed.), *The Faber Book of Pop* (Faber & Faber, 1995)

Hilary Kingsley & Geoff Tibballs, *Box of Delights: The Golden Years of Television* (MacMillan, 1989)

Bernard Levin, *The Pendulum Years: Britain and the Sixties* (Jonathan Cape, 1970; pbk edn: Pan, 1972)

Richard Mabey, *The Pop Process* (Hutchinson, 1969)

George Melly, *Revolt Into Style: The Pop Arts in Britain* (Allen Lane, 1970)

John Mortimer, *Paradise Postponed* (Viking, 1985; pbk edn: Penguin, 1986)

Simon Napier-Bell, *You Don't Have to Say You Love Me* (New English Library, 1982)

Andrew Loog Oldham, *Stoned* (Secker & Warburg, 2000; pbk edn: Vintage, 2001)

Joe Orton (ed. John Lahr), *The Orton Diaries* (Methuen, 1986; pbk edn: 1987)

David Owen, *Time to Declare* (Michael Joseph, 1991; pbk edn: Penguin, 1992)

Jeremy Pascall (ed.), *The Story of Pop* (part-work, Phoebus, 1974–76)

Private Eye, *Private Pop Eye: The Life and Times of Spiggy Topes, Or Not* (Pressdram, 1969)

Griff Rhys Jones, *Semi-Detached* (Michael Joseph, 2006; pbk edn: Penguin, 2007)

John Robb, *The North Will Rise Again: Manchester Music City 1976–1996* (Aurum, 2009)

David Roberts (ed.), *The Guinness Book of British Hit Singles* (1977; 14th edition: Guinness World Records, 2001)

Mick Rock & David Bowie, *Moonage Daydream: The Life and Times of Ziggy Stardust* (Cassell Illustrated, 2005; orig. pub. Genesis Publications, 2002)

Francis Rossi & Rick Parfitt, with Mick Wall, *XS All Areas: The Status Quo Autobiography* (Sidgwick & Jackson, 2004; pbk edn: Pan, 2005)

Anthony Scaduto, *Bob Dylan* (W.H. Allen, 1972; pbk edn: Abacus, 1972)

Joe Smith (ed. Mitchell Fink), *Off the Record: An Oral History of Popular Music* (Sidgwick & Jackson, 1989; pbk edn: Pan, 1990)

Julian Symons, *Bloody Murder: From the Detective Story to the Crime Novel – a History* (Faber & Faber, 1972; rev pbk edn: Penguin, 1974)

Harry Thompson, *Peter Cook: A Biography* (Hodder & Stoughton, 1997; pbk edn: Sceptre, 1998)

Alwyn W. Turner, *The Biba Experience* (Antique Collectors Club, 2004)

Alwyn W. Turner, *Crisis? What Crisis? Britain in the 1970s* (Aurum, 2008)

Richard Unterberer, *Turn! Turn! Turn! The '60s Folk-Rock Revolution* (Backbeat, 2002)

John Walker, *Bluff Your Way in Social Climbing* (Wolfe Publishing, 1967)

Johnnie Walker, *The Autobiography* (Michael Joseph, 2007; pbk edn: Penguin, 2008)

Joel Whitburn, *The Billboard Book of USA Top 40 Albums* (Billboard Publications, 1987)

Joel Whitburn, *The Billboard Book of USA Top 40 Hits* (Record Research, 1989)

Ian Whitcomb, *After the Ball* (Allen Lane, 1972; pbk edn: Penguin, 1973)

Harold Wilson, *The New Britain: Labour's Plan – Selected Speeches 1964* (Penguin, 1964)

Acknowledgements

Firstly, this project would never have made it out of the starting blocks without the enthusiasm, commitment and co-operation of Harry Goodwin himself and of John O'Connor.

I'm greatly indebted to the following, who were kind enough to provide assistance in various ways: Adrian Perkins, Alan Johnson, Bill Wyman, Bobby Elliott, Chris Spedding, Colin Blunstone, Daryl Easlea, Dave Hill, Dick Greener, Eric Aniversario, Herbie Flowers, John Briggs, John Flaxman, John McConnell, John Sebastian, Jonathan King, Ken Adler, Ken Knox, Les McKeown, Michelle Coomber, Mike McCartney, Nicholas Henderson, Nigel Stanworth, Peter Noone, Phil Wainman, Ray Dorset, Roger Crimlis, Ron Roker, Sheila Bowen, Sid Smith, Stanley Dorfman, Steve Ellis, Steve Thomas, Suzi Quatro, Terry Christian, Tony Brown, Tony Burrows, Trevor Bolder and Wendy Burton.

Obviously none of the above should be considered to condone the contents of this book. Apologies too to everyone whose work I've quoted in such a cavalier fashion, probably missing all the important points.

I'd also like to thank Clare Davis, Clare Faulkner, Geoff Barlow, Julie Chan and Sam Safer in V&A Publishing, and Geoffrey Marsh, Victoria Broackes, Sara Nuzzi and Stuart Aird in V&A Theatre Collections.

Thamasin Marsh has been a great source of support during this project.

And finally my thanks, as ever, to the other members of the Wrecking Crew: Mark Eastment, Isobel Gillan and Clare Collinson.

The chapter titles are taken from the titles of hits for Gerry and the Pacemakers, Georgie Fame and the Blue Flames, Donovan, the Jimi Hendrix Experience, the Who, Mary Hopkin and Rod Stewart.

Index

First published by V&A Publishing, 2010

Distributed in North America by Harry N. Abrams, Inc., New York

© 2010 Alwyn W. Turner
(www.alwynturner.com)

ISBN 978 185177 5972
Library of Congress Control Number 20099322295

10 9 8 7 6 5 4 3 2 1
2014 2013 2012 2011 2010

A catalogue record for this book is available from the British Library.

Designer: Isobel Gillan
Copy-editor: Clare Collinson

Front jacket/cover illustration: Elton John
Back jacket/cover illustration: Jimi Hendrix

PAGE 1: Aretha Franklin; PAGES 2–3: Ron Wood and Rod Stewart of the Faces; PAGES 4–5: John Lennon; PAGE 240: Pan's People.

Printed in Singapore

V&A Publishing
Victoria and Albert Museum
South Kensington
London SW7 2RL
www.vam.ac.uk

The following dates for the photographs in *My Generation* were compiled by the author, journalist and archive film and video researcher, Keith Badman (www.keithbadman.com/).

p.1: Aug 1968; pp.2–3: Nov 1972; pp.4–5: Apr 1965; p.6: Dec 1968; p.9: 1963; p.10: Jan 1966; pp.12, 13: Jul 1969; p.14: Feb 1967; p.17: Aug 1966; p.19: Dec 1969; p.20: May 1964; p.21: Feb 1964; p.22: May 1965; p.23l: Jan 1965; p.23r: Mar 1964; p.24t: Nov 1969; p.24b: Aug 1965; p.25: Nov 1966; pp.26, 27: Oct 1964; pp.28–29, 30: Jun 1966; p.31: Jul 1964; p.32: c. 1964; p.34: Jul 1965; p.35: Mar 1967; pp.36–7: c. 1965; p.38: Jul 1964; p.39: Oct 1964; pp.40–1: Feb 1966; p.42: Feb 1964; p.43: Feb 1964; p.44: Dec 1968; p.45: Jan 1964; p.46: Dec 1964; p.47: Jul 1964; p.48: Feb 1964; p.49t: Feb 1964; p.49b: Feb 1970; p.51: Jun 1965; pp.53, 54–5: Dec 1965; pp.56l&r: Jun 1964; pp.57, 58, 59: Jun 1964; pp.60–1: Dec 1964; p.62: Aug 1964; p.63l: Jun 1966; p.63r: Nov 67; p.64: Jan 1964; p.65: Nov 1965; p.66: Mar 1965; p.67l, c&r: Nov 1965; p.68: Jan 1965; p.69: Jun 1966; p.70: c. Jan 1964; p.71: Oct 1965; p.72t&b: Jul 1966; p.73: Oct 1966; p.74: Aug 1964; p.75: Mar 1965; p.76: Sept 1969; pp.78–9: Jan 1964; p.81: Oct 1964; p.82: Feb 1965; p.83: Aug 1964; p.85: Jun 1965; p.86: Aug 1965; p.87: Aug 1965; p.88: Mar 1965; p.89l: Aug 1966; p.89r: May 1966; p.91: Nov 1964; p.92: Apr 1966; p.93: Jul 1966; p.94tl: Apr 1965; p.94–5: Dec 1965; p.96l: Feb 1965; p.96r: Apr 1966; p.97: Feb 1971; pp.98, 99: May 1965; p.100t: Aug 1964; p.100b: Feb 1968; pp.100–01: Sept 1971; p.102: Aug 1967; p.103: Jan 1968; pp.104t, 104–5: May 1971; p.104b: May 1971; p.106: Jul 1972; p.107t: Jan 1972; p.107b: May 1970; p.108: Dec 1972; p.109l: Sept 1971; p.109r: Nov 1972; p.111: Apr 1967; p.112: Mar 1965; pp.114l&r, 115: Nov 1966; p.116tr: Dec 1966; p.116bl: Jun 1967; p.117: Dec 1966; p.118: Dec 1966; p.119: May 1967; pp.120–1: Jan 1967; pp.122, 123: Jul 1969; p.124: Mar 1967; p.126: Jan 1967; p.127: Jul 1967; p.128tl: Dec 1967; pp.128–9: May 1967; p.130: Dec 1967; p.131: Oct 1967; p.132: Oct 1967; p.134l: May 1966; p.134r: Sept 1967; p.135: Oct 1967; pp.136–7: Feb 1968; p.138l: Jan 1964; p.138r: Oct 1967; p.139: Mar 1970; p.141: Feb 1969; p.142l: Jun 1969; p.142r: Sept 1970; p.143: Feb 1970; pp.144, 145: Oct 1969; p.146: May 1969; p.147: Jan 1970; p.148: Jul 1969; p.149l: Jan 1973; p.149r: Jan 1972; p.150: Sept 1968; p.151: c. 1974; p.152: Jun 1970; p.153: Jun 1971; p.154bl: Feb 1970; pp.154–5: Feb 1973; p.156: Mar 1970; p.157: Feb 1970; pp.158–61: Dec 1971; pp.162–3: Dec 1970; p.164: Sept 1970; p.165: Aug 1971; p.166l: Oct 1970; p.166r: Dec 1973; p.167: Nov 1972; pp.168tl: Mar 1970; pp.168–9: Nov 1972; p.170: May 1972; p.172: Feb 1973; p.173: c. 1974; p.175: Sept 1971; p.176: Aug 1970; p.178t: Jan 1971; p.178b: Jan 1969; p.179: Nov 1972; pp.180–1: Jun 1971; p.181tr: Sept 1972; p.181br: Feb 1970; p.182: Aug 1971; p.184l: Jan 1971; p.184r: Mar 1973; p.185: Aug 1973; p.186: Jun 1968; p.187: Sept 1967; pp.188–9, 190–1: Nov 1972; p.193: Nov 1972; pp.194–5: Jun 1971; p.195: Jun 1968; p.197: c. 1971; pp.198–9: Apr 1970; p.199br: Aug 1974; p.200: Nov 1971; p.201: Apr 1971; p.202l: Nov 1972; p.202c: Aug 1972; p.202r: Jun 1971; p.203: Aug 1970; pp.204–05: Jan 1968; p.207: Aug 1972; p.208: Nov 1970; p.209: Jun 1970; p.210l: Mar 1976; pp.210–11: May 1972; p.212: Apr 1975; p.213: Nov 1972; pp.214, 215: Jul 1972; pp.216–17: Jul 1972; p.218: Nov 1973; p.219: Dec 1972; pp.220, 221: Sept 1972; p.222: Dec 1972; p.223: Sept 1972; pp.224, 225: Jan 1973; pp.226–7: Apr 1972; p.228: Nov 1973; p.229l: Nov 1973; p.229r: May 1974; p.230: Sept 1971; p.233: May 1972; p.240: c. 1971.